Beautiful Mess

A Journey to the Universe Within

Created by Barb Heite

Through journaling with My Real Love Coach

Sharon Winningham...

She read each and every journal entry...

April 2013 - April 2014

Amor De Soi Publishing-Scottsdale, AZ 85250

Copyright © 2014 by Barbara Heite

Amor De Soi Publishing is a trademark of Amor De Soi, LLC

Published 2014

Concept Cover Design: Emma Wilkerson

Cover Design: Heart Centered Media

Editor: Joan Schaublin

Text Design: Heart Centered Media

Disclaimer:

The intent of the author is only to share information of a general nature to help you in your quest for emotional and spiritual well-being. In the event you use any of the information in this book for yourself, which is your constitutional right, the author and the publisher assume no responsibility for your actions.

To protect the privacy, names have been omitted

Printed in the United States of America

Library of Congress Control Number: 2014914762

Heite, Barbara

Beautiful Mess . . . A Journey to the Universe Within/

Barb Heite

p. cm.

ISBN: 978-0692273265

1. Self-acceptance. 2. Self-realization 3. Self-esteem. 4. Intuition 5. Spirituality

I. Title.

Trade paper ISBN-13: 978-0692273265

"I Love You to The Moon and Back" . . . her children with a giggle, carefree, easy-breezy child-like openness said in unison to her as each chose their path to discover and explore...

And she stopped, and looked at each of them . . . really *looked* . . . and she saw love . . . unconditional love in her children . . . and she, with a feeling of a blessed heart . . . with mistiness of joy and love in her eyes.... Whispered into the wind as each went on their journey, into the adventures we call life . . .

"I Love You to the Moon and Back...and even more deeply and simply.... You are in my heart....wherever you may roam"...

Daja, Kevon, and Arianna....

You are beautiful . . . amazing, lovely . . . brave, courageous, caring, thoughtful, compassionate human beings . . . I have learned and grown so much from being your mom . . . I am truly blessed and forever grateful that you chose me to be your mom...

Love, Love ♥

For Sharon...my Real Love Coach
Anam Cara

*W*ith a glance, kind word, loving embrace . . . an instant bond, connection created . . . and I know that you *see* me . . . I instantly shift to being open, sensitive, and vulnerable in those moments . . . I catch my breath . . . understanding that you chose to stop your world for me . . . My heart touched and appreciative, relaxed, feeling wanted. I release my breath . . . and shift from the murkiness of my wandering mind . . . so I can *see* through the obscurity . . . continually moving toward reality, clarity, centeredness, knowing the only way out is through . . . I stand my ground and walk through it all . . . and I emerge from the vagueness of my drifting thoughts and feelings to clarity . . . and I can *see* how beautiful you are . . . from the inside-out . . . sensing, absorbing, being encircled in your grace, love, kindness, and tenderness . . . and I become misty eyed with the realization that I know you love me . . . not limited by separation, distance, or time . . . open to accepting, understanding ALL parts of me . . . not just fragments of me . . . I experience awareness felt by the heart . . . awakened . . . transcending physical space . . . attuned to the eternal flow of humanity . . . love . . . felt deeply within my personal universe . . . the self-universe we each carry within us, continually shaping, influencing, listening to promptings, encouraged from the inside out . . . when in harmony with my internal vibration . . . connecting with other "worlds" . . . knowing, feeling divine grace . . . carrying each one toward our callings . . . creating a path and practicing and noticing our and others internal light . . . giving and receiving . . . creating comfort . . . to relax and breathe, giving encouragement to be creative, loving, self . . . sharing wisdom, knowings, expanding, evolving . . . to being authentically, naturally self . . . generous and receptive . . . in accepting all . . . in kindness, tenderness, compassion . . . and unconditional love . . . understanding we are all more than what is on the surface . . . and that ALL have gifts to share . . . in inspired loving moments, I know that I am BLESSED and HONORED, GRATEFUL . . . to have what is called an ANAM CARA . . . a connection at the soul level . . . a soul friend to share with...

CONTENTS

PREFACE

*I*n my writings I often refer to Real Love. I wanted to give a short explanation as to the understanding of what Real Love is. With my Real Love Life Coach, Sharon Winningham, this is a short description of Real Love:

Real Love is a teaching of guiding principles that once applied we feel more connection, intimacy and more love in all of our relationships. Based on a series of books written by Dr. Greg Baer, these teachings have taken on a grassroots trickle down to people all over the world. The teaching is helping people replace fear and confusion with peace and confidence. Its core premise is that we all need unconditional love and without it, we have a terrible void in our lives. Sharon Winningham, CRLC of Phoenix began the first major efforts of spreading these guiding principles to others and now there are people all over the world practicing loving and teaching others.

If you would like additional detailed information on Real Love you can go to these links.

Dr. Greg Baer

www.realllove.com

Sharon Winningham, CRCL

www.sharonawinningham.com

www.meetup.com/reallove

www.reallove.com

In addition, I wanted to share that I purposely left the writings *as is* . . . or as close as possible . . . because this is how the words flowed from me to share with my Real Love Coach, Sharon Winningham . . . While walking my journey through Real Love. I do not want to take away from being authentically me . . . with the misspelled words, wrong use of grammar, and any other *mistakes* found…it does not matter when you look beyond the details and feel with your heart…

These parts of my heart are from the prospective of my perception of my world as I experienced. I started working with Sharon the week I was

1

diagnosed with cancer at 46 years of age with my 26 year marriage unraveling. With courage and a lot of support from the Real Love Community I finally took time to stop to breathe, listen to within . . . and chose to walk through the pain to the light to stand in LOVE . . . .

My intention is to share my inner world . . . not paint another world as black . . . meaning, I clearly understand that those we love and interact daily with are human and make choices that affect others . . . creating ripple effects of energy . . . and I have come to awareness that we all are just perfect the way we are, with human flaws, gifts to learn and grow from. We also are Divine Beings and are blessed with the capacity to comprehend choices . . . creating beautiful messes . . . experiencing, tripping, stumbling, and falling into what is waiting within . . . The Truth . . . that each of us matter, are important, and contribute to the universal truth when our hearts open to connect and twine to stand in our inherent power firmly rooted in the Truth . . . that WE ARE ALL LOVE . . . the rest is just stories . . . details . . .

Love leaves a significant mark…and nothing will ever be the same again…

WRITINGS OF A JOURNEY
FROM THE OUTSIDE, IN…

*A*s the reader, you can choose to start from the End, the INSIDE, and read entries to the OUTSIDE, the journey from within…from back to front…or vice-versa from the Outward to Inward…or just open and start reading . . . Really, there is no wrong way to read this…whatever makes you happy . . . your choice . . . your journey . . . I simply love you no matter what you choose . . . I feel blessed to share my heart with you . . . connecting . . . humbly . . . beautifully…

Enjoy…

Love, Love

PASSAGES

UNCONDITIONAL LOVE...REAL LOVE

*T*here are people who enter our lives that forever create a transformation within us . . . we are blessed with our children, family, and cherished friends . . . then there are those once in a lifetime encounters with what I call "earth angels." They know their purpose and share their talents with others unconditionally; guiding, encouraging, teaching others to *see* their worth; that each of us matter; that each of us are loved beyond measure and *are* love . . . softening our hearts, encouraging each of us to grow, stretch and *see* beyond the details and illusions of our daily life; to *see* who each of us are. A contribution, a treasure, a gift to the whole, contributing to the universal soul of us all, expanding, creating ripple effects that touch everything...ever expanding into consciousness.. Into what only really matters...unconditional love . . .

ANGELS

*T*his is for all the Angels in my life . . . and there are many . . . but one in particular . . . no matter where I am . . . how my life unfolds . . . I can close my eyes and feel her presence with me . . . she is in my heart right alongside my children . . . and brothers and sister . . . she encourages me to be me . . . and I can just be Me *with* her . . . I love her heart, the bravery to be just her . . . the courage to be uniquely herself . . . and encouraging others to just *be* also . . . accepting of others and herself when tripping, sometimes crawling and falling . . . through our beautiful messes we call our lives . . . Simply put . . . I love her . . . and all Angels . . . which means All of you...

This could not be . . . if not for the unconditional love and support I received from the Real Love community, my friends, family, and most of all, Sharon...

I Love You to the Moon and Back...and even more deeply and simply...

The truth I know in my heart to be true:

4

I love you in this moment and beyond, inward to my Being, expanding outward to share with you and all others...I simply love you...

JUST ME

*T*oday I am happy; mostly because I went down to the hospital and spoke with the education RN. She spent an hour with me answering all of my questions and made me feel welcome. I am struggling with the fact that I am not as sick as most of the people there. The nurse said I was very welcome to be there; I was allowing them to help me and know that the outcome would be good. She said to think of it as a gift I was giving to them to get to work with me. Just hearing that lifted most of my anxiety and feeling like a burden. I really feel like they care for my wellbeing. I also got to talk with a wellness coach who gave me some breathing exercises and grounding exercises to practice, so when I am overwhelmed and anxious, I can calm myself. We talked about my self-talk and how I should also use this method when I am "attacking" myself. I will try to be more aware of it so I can practice.

My teenage life with my mom was short lived. She mostly dumped us off at friends' homes, or she would leave and we would end up back in foster care for a while, and then back to her . . . She always called me names, especially "a prick teaser" when I was around twelve to fourteen, but I had no idea what that was. I was so scared of boys and men that my husband is the only person I have been with, because I trust him not to take of advantage of me. When I was about fifteen, the verbal abuse was just out of control. I ignored it. When I was sixteen, I stayed with my dad for nine months, and then he moved away and I chose to stay in California. From that point on, I have been doing it all myself . . . I worked two jobs and went to school until I graduated. When I was nineteen, I knew I needed help . . . so I sued the person who molested me to pay for my counseling. I was called a liar and told that I just wanted attention.

I just wanted to be okay.

When my husband gets angry I feel sooooo small, and I just want to

5

fix whatever is wrong so he won't be mad at me. I want him to love me so much that I give him control of me. Working on that . . . I think his anger stems from not feeling loved by his mom and dad. He is so scared that he has to control with anger. I do get scared when he is super angry because he does not know how to calm himself down, which ultimately shuts me down. I give him his space and let him calm down, and speak with him a few days later. He tells me how I feel, and how I do everything wrong, and, "Why can't you just..." I then get scared and frustrated because the rules change at his whim and I can't keep it straight. I am afraid to say anything, because I am afraid of it being wrong, yet again. Then sometimes I just don't care and I either let it all out or shut him out. I can't fix him, nor do I want to, because it is just enough to work on me.

I am on a journey and have a purpose. I believe that I am where I am supposed to be for a reason; even though I may not know what that reason is.

Regards

INFORMATION

*T*oday I am sitting in contentment. Just doing my thing and not stressing so much.

Sharon asked me to Journal to her and let her know the emotions I had about my sexual abuse..............

On my own from almost seventeen on. That is when I was able to stop the sexual abuse. The person who abused me is such an angry person. He was also arrogant and mean. He called me baby Shamu when I was about twelve to fourteen (puberty). I was probably about 10 pounds heavier than I should have been, but by the time I was reaching sixteen I was too thin. As mean as he was to me, he was even meaner to my sister. I don't know why. My sister and I never talked about the sexual abuse except to make a promise never to tell because we did not want to upset the family.

(What were we thinking?)

I should also add that my mom's boyfriends would constantly make sexually explicit comments about me from about thirteen on. One actually crawled into bed with me and told me all the sexual acts he would do to me if I would let him, but I didn't; probably why my mom was always calling me names. I was the most reserved, uptight kid, but that did not stop the comments.

When I was sixteen (I still can't believe this happened), a man literally pulled me off my bike when I was riding it to work and pulled me into his car and started kissing me. I would not lift my legs up for him to shut the door. Somehow I was able to wiggle out from underneath him and I ran into the restaurant whose parking lot this took place in.

The hostess thought we were just a couple having a fight and did not want to interfere. I just waited for him to leave to go to work. I did not have anyone to talk to and just broke down in front of everyone at work and was asked to go home and get myself together. I was so grateful that I was not fired. Now, looking back, I can't believe that I did not call the police and people just didn't want to deal with it to help me. It was very isolating for me when I think about it.

When I was dating Him I was upfront about my childhood and all the stuff I had been through. He basically stated that if I didn't get help to work out my stuff, He did not know if we could get married. Then I got pregnant. I don't even know if He remembers saying that. All I thought was that I was not going to let my childhood affect my future. I did not have any money so I decided to sue the person who molested me.

Just to back track a little, my sister wanted to literally kill me when I decided to let everyone know the truth, but she supported me. It was weird for me; I actually almost withdrew the suit because my family was telling me that I would financially ruin the person who molested me. My sister was in Alaska on remote, but decided to go ahead and continue the suit, so I pushed forward. I had to do all the leg work myself because she was not there at the beginning. I was really worried about hurting certain people in my family. Eventually, we did settle when we were twenty-one. I had just had my 1st child. I used the money for counseling.

The first time I went to counseling I worked on my self-image and learning how to love myself (still working on that). The second time I

7

worked on my guilt over hurting my family by suing and bringing this out into the open. That is when I came to an understanding that there was no way certain people could have not known what was going on . . . they simply ignored it because of their own fear . . . I always looked at these people, these family members, as victims of this broken person who was so selfish in his actions; controlling and attacking with no thought to others . . . but they were not strong enough to stand up and fight him; they had shattered spirits. I, wanting to be accepted, always had a story to tell myself about the reasons why no one could love me just then . . . And I gave myself permission to be patient a little bit longer . . . Then my heart would be seen . . . my love felt . . . And shared . . . Little girl dreams . . . I dreamed so big sometimes . . . Since then, I have done counseling off and on over the years. I first focused on me, and then it shifted toward our marriage . . . then back and forth. I have taken many classes, read more books than I care to admit, and finally this. It has been such a long road.

I still think about my relationship with Him a lot . . . waiting for the other shoe to drop . . . It is hard to get over that feeling . . . but how I adore that man!

Thanks for reading

SAD

My feelings . . . today I woke up sad and became sadder . . . just a sense of sadness, probably because I am thinking about all this stuff. Once I got to work I was able to shift to feeling contentment; then it was fine.

My emotions about the person who molested me . . . very disconnected with that. I let that go a long time ago. It has been over 10 years since I even attempted to connect.

My molester's spouse for whatever reason, I just loved so much. She was kind to me and mean to him so I really connected with that when I was younger. As I grew older, I realized that she lived in victimhood, and liked the attention from that. I also realized when I was older that she was a very sad lady; you could see it in her eyes. I think

8

that is why I did not want to hurt her anymore; because I could see in her eyes that she was so sad and defeated. I just had this understanding about her. I did not want to add to her pain.

Later, I did not have a choice but to realize that she had to have known what he was doing, and continued to let it happen. That was a wake-up call for me when I had the realization that this was a sick woman, and no matter how much I loved her, I could not love her enough to give her what she needed. She was broken and had given in. I decided to disconnect from her in one sudden swoop; I thought that would be easier for her. I don't know how she felt about me after that, nor did I care. I mourned her at that time and moved forward.

I do not know all that she experienced because she did not share it. Stories from here and there came to me, and her husband was just a bastard and a self-centered and self-serving individual. He destroyed people and did not even blink an eye at his own cruelty, or acknowledge the damage that was done.

My feeling about my molester is that he is a lonely, old, bitter man. I know this because my family occasionally updates me on his wellbeing. I am glad that he is living to be old and has to live with all he's done. It probably does not faze him because I am projecting how I would act in that situation, but it does make me hope that he has a slight understanding of what he has done. I am not angry, sad, or anything concerning him. I know what was done are his actions to own, not mine. I had no control over the situation. I do struggle and have triggers and I try to talk myself through them, but it does cause me to struggle to cope with certain situations.

I have this irrational fear of being attacked while I sleep because of the experiences in my childhood. I seem to cycle through these sleep patterns wherein it is extremely hard for me to fall asleep and stay asleep; especially when I have a lot of stress or anxiety, like now.

My approach is to do what I need to do to get back to a lower stress level in order to feel better again.

Thanks

RELATIONSHIPS

I do not want to see the person who molested me, and his spouse died in 2010.

When she got mad at her husband, the man who molested me, it was because he did something to her; it had nothing to do with the kids. They were really verbally abusive to each other. She put a lot of energy into appearing proper, and she never once said one bad thing to me about him. I would hear them communicate in the car or through the walls, and every once in a while in front of me. She never yelled; she just became upset and kind of rigid when she was dealing with her husband. We never spoke about him or what he was doing to me, so no connection there. I probably read more into her actions, because I saw her as someone who loved me.

I never want to be viewed as a victim so I worked hard on not being a victim, which means I don't share many feelings. This is an issue with Him and me …when He is angry or judging, He will state, "You are in your victim role," or martyr role, or whatever he thinks I am doing at the moment.

So, I try not to talk about things that bother me because He will point out the role I am currently in. I feel like He is judging instead of listening.

In the relationship with my molester's wife, I never stopped caring, but I had to mourn our relationship as if she was dead already. I stopped missing her after the first few years. It was the only way to move forward with this part of my life. It was not an easy decision for me, or one I made lightly. I thought about it and talked extensively with my sister and a therapist. I wanted to make sure I was not running from the relationship, but coming to a healthy conclusion. I know that I made the right choice. I did the same with my mom. I love her and wish her well, but the relationship was not one of sharing but rather of controlling on her part.

I also talked to my mom, as did my brother, as to the boundaries that she needed to follow to have a relationship with me. She chose not to respect those boundaries . . . so I chose not to have a relationship with her.

My feelings for these relationships are just neutral when I hear news of what is going on with these family members. I can sometimes feel compassion for them as they walk their journeys. When people are sharing stories about the people I chose not to have in my life, I truly understand the emotional stress they feel because I am there . . . I don't mind if they come up in conversation with family, because it is the natural flow of the conversation. I do not get upset; I simply just listen and let it be. I really have no emotional connection to those people and don't really care at this point what they might be struggling through.

You are right that I physically react to certain smells or clothing on men (mostly robes), and to hearing footsteps in the hall or having the sense that I am being watched in my sleep (that part sucks). I get triggered and I start having anxiety about sleeping.

So the sexual abuse always happened at night. He would come in after I would fall asleep and wake me up or I would wake up and there he was; very freaky.

With others, they would come and pull me out of bed in a rage and rip me out of sleep, screaming and beating the crap out of me over some minor detail like not washing the dishes correctly.

LAST NIGHT

I am tired. I talked to my manager today about cutting back on my hours through the summer. I'm waiting for the necessary paper work (started process).

Last night I could not sleep again because this random memory that I had not thought of popped into my head. It was about my step-brother.

I remember this; he locked my sister and I in a room by tying two hallway doors together so you couldn't open either door. The windows had bars. He told us he was going to set the house on fire with us in it. I remember I was so panicked because he would have done it if someone hadn't come home. That same day I packed a backpack and left. I contacted my mom and she said that he was only playing with us and that she was going to stay there. I was fifteen, a few months from sixteen.

My sister and I walked about 20 miles. I can't remember what happened during that day long walk, I just remember ending up back in Carlsbad where we had lived previously, and we talked to our old Bishop. I do not know how he convinced my dad, who also lived in Carlsbad, to take me and my sister in, but he did for about 9 months. It was such a turbulent time in my life. I also know, as bad as it seemed, I was almost done dealing with all these people who disregarded me as a kid. I had hope for the future; it was like leaving prison. I did not care what it took to escape it and stay away from it. All the suffering and hurt was in my past; so I thought. I could move forward because I knew my sister and brothers were safe as well. It was a journey that separated us, but we came back together many years later.

The stuff that happened before I even became a teenager is mind boggling. I have totally separated myself from that kid; she's like another person in my mind's eye. I wonder how we pulled through all this stuff . . . I sometimes wonder what purpose this childhood served. Such a total lack of care for another person is very confusing for me. I think that is why I have a hard time with people struggling (hurting), because I know how isolated and afraid they are. I can see it in people's eyes; I don't want to see the pain. I try to offer comfort, but I know, and they know, it is not enough. The journey to happiness is from within, and for some the journey just feels too hard to take. So I listen and support. That is all for now...

I KNEW...

*T*oday I am feeling discouraged and overwhelmed.

I spoke with someone on the phone today and we talked about my mom and Him.

With my mom, I am fine with the relationship, but have a hard time speaking out loud that I do not like her. I make excuses for her behavior to minimize her actions. I also do this with Him.

I knew I was clingy, but Lordy, I am really clingy. I do not like to admit this at all. I am fighting the urge to give up because it is really hard for me to see me in this light. I know I have to be able to see it, and I think I always have, but just didn't pay attention to the signs because I did not want to deal with it and what it might mean for me. It is hard to think about.

I am uncertain of what is going to be and I just kinda want to roll with it and not fight it. I am just feeling that way today. I don't know where I'll be tomorrow.

Peace out.

THAT'S IT

I am really tired today.

I am still feeling discouraged, but it might be due to the fact that I am tired and don't have much energy today.

I got really frustrated with someone at work today because she would not stop whining about how people don't like her. I told her not to let other people's judgments rule her. Then I asked her if she thought she was rude. She said, "No." I said, "I don't see an issue then." I told her to be professionally polite. She said, "I do not understand because I am liked by everybody." I am not, but I did not share that with her. I told her she is putting too much pressure on herself to make others happy. No matter what I said she went back to, "You just don't understand," and I went to, "It is your choice as to how to behave; own it." I do not know why I felt the need to enlighten her in anyway.

My patience gets tested when people are blatantly in a negative frame of mind and telling me I don't understand. It irritates me because people just assume I don't understand. Another girl at work also stated that I had a charmed life and wished she'd had the same opportunities I had. I do not go into what I have, but really? One thing I know is that most people who seem to have a charmed life have it because of the effort they put into it. Very few people see the struggle to get there. Success is not measured in money but from the inside out. I try not to go into it at work, because most people just don't care to understand where I have been, how far I have come, and how far I have to go. The only difference between me and them is my willingness to at least try and not give up. That is it. I just try one way, and if that doesn't work, I will try another. The flip side of success is failure. It is how each of us handles failure that will determine our success. That's it.

Peace out.

FIXING

I apologized today after I read your comments. I told her I was sorry for not acknowledging her feelings and that I should not have told her how to feel about it. That is all I got out before she went on a 10 minute dump about how awful her life was, so I just tried to end it politely (I have to work with her).

I try not to talk or get to involved (cornered) because all she can do is talk about how hurt she is, and I don't have the energy to deal with it.

I did not make any calls today because I did not want to talk with anyone about anything. I just wanted to be and not share.

Pretending to be nice; I was not pretending, and I was not particularly nice either. It is how I feel and think. Each person has a choice as to how he or she interacts with the world. I know feelings (emotions) can become confusing, but we internally have the choice and accountability for our actions. My issue is fixing; it is ingrained, but I am becoming more aware of it.

I am also frustrated at Him right now because He does not walk the walk with Real Love.

I know I am judging. He does not make His calls. He said he would go to the group meeting, then didn't. We talked about it briefly. I am at, "Who cares?" His dedication is already fading . . . like so many times before. He got me excited about this and now I feel like I am doing it alone (at least today).

These are just thoughts running through my head . . . I really am feeling disconnected and that scares me as well.

Oh so negative lately . . . makes me sad.

MOVING ON . . .

*T*he lady at work; I cannot catch a break with her. I know you said to tell her that I cannot help her but she is quick to jump in . . . and the relationship, for the most part, is not worth all the effort to let her know I don't have it in me to listen to her talk about her hurts. I know this is running, but really, I do not value our relationship and have to work with her in a team capacity. I will be professionally polite, but I do not want to attempt yet again (at least not now) to tell her I can't listen to her (that is one of her biggest complaints; that no one cares). I am going to let it be, and if this situation comes up I will try to be upfront with her about not being able to listen to her right now.

Moving on . . .

I am a big jumbly mess of emotions. I am feeling like I am not being supportive of Him. I am having a hard time talking about this with Him because I do not want to say the wrong thing and hurt His feelings or make him feel like I do not love Him or care.

I want Him to be okay. I want to be okay. I want us to be okay. But, I don't feel okay . . . just here . . .

Still in a negative frame of mind...

Peace out.

DISCONNECTED

I went to the meeting today. I shared a little . . . I still feel disconnected. I am still processing our session.

I just do not want to communicate with anyone because I just feel like I am not being heard correctly. I was taken aback when He brought up this whole situation about the thing with our daughter; only because we spoke about it at length with our previous therapist and He spoke to me on several occasions in private. I understand that there must still be feelings around this incident that have not been resolved for Him.

I am also surprised to hear that I am clingy and being passive aggressive because I told Him I was going to do something else. I understand that the tone in which it was said is important, but I did not say it in an accusing way. I was merely letting Him know where I was going because on past occasions when I just left the room and he did not notice until later, He thought I was mad at him; I wasn't and told Him so.

I am feeling more disconnected than ever and right now I am feeling like I don't care, which I keep telling myself, "That is not true. I do care. I just don't want to care." I am sorta confused with this whole communication thing with Him and others.

I am feeling like I have done a lot of damage because of the way I have communicated with Him and I am having a hard time fighting the victimhood in this. I logically understand, but man, my emotions are just telling me otherwise.

Like, I have the right to be upset about the past hurts in my life, but then my logical side is telling me that I am overreacting and being a drama queen. I know I should let it out and I guess that is what I am trying to do, but I am scared that by opening up I will be judged and told I am wrong...

So after reading this back, I am in victimhood, because I am going along and not speaking up for myself . . . making excuses to minimize accountability . . . running because I am escaping inside myself and sleeping more than I should and avoiding people . . . clingy because I have this desire to just go on and on to prove myself . . . attacking because I want to be right and feel like I need to defend myself.

I do not really like having to see myself this way so blaringly. I am feeling very inadequate...

Sometimes being aware of oneself just kinda sucks.

I am feeling defeated. Right at this moment I do not want to connect with anyone, which is the most wrong thing to do . . . but that is how I feel.

Peace out.

WANT

So I probably should not have brought up this whole situation with the money. I asked Him about it and I let Him talk and I listened; and then I responded. All He heard was that He was wrong. I accepted that I did not act in His best interest, and that I was trying to look like the "good guy" again, as always (His words). I understand that this is how He sees it, and I acknowledged those feelings. I also said I was surprised that He still felt this strongly about the whole situation, so He felt attacked. I just made Him feel worse, and then He said we do not know how to communicate ever. I am feeling defeated. He said I don't understand. I feel like He says that to discount what I am saying, which gives Him the right to beat me up with His tone and then shut me down. He was very upset, which made my stomach hurt (acting like a victim . . . maybe . . . it was a physical reaction). I wanted to defend myself . . . but I tried not to, though he said I was. I wanted clarity but became confused. I stated that the details don't really matter, but how He felt did. That we could argue for days about what we each did or did not do. I am truly sorry . . . but He said that that was not true, and that He was not ready to accept my apologies. I am in a quandary, because I am really, really, surprised by how hurt He still feels about this whole mess. I am beginning to think it is not the situation that happened, but the inferior feelings He has toward Himself. I don't know. I really do not know what to say to Him about this. I do not know how to express any more clearly how sorry I am for making Him feel so betrayed. I am just super stuck on this.

I am sitting there feeling this, and I am not feeling good, and I just want to escape Him because I do not want to feel that (running). I am scared that He will leave me (clingy). I told Him I needed a break. I tried to call you; only you, though . . . just did not want to explain (acting like a victim). I am super splashing trying to stay above water right now. I want to do this right. I want Him to be happy and I am afraid of how He will define what that looks like.

I am so co-dependent and my urge is to cling tighter or run and not look back. I know I must walk through this. I know I can do this. I want to do this. I want to be happy all the time. I want the best for Him . . . and me too. I went outside and just cried a little, and tried to pull myself together. I should have called more than just you but right now I am struggling with the phone calls. I don't want to share, just hide (victimhood), but I am committed to either reading the book or watching the DVD's daily.

I don't want to be clingy, but I am. I don't want to be a victim, but I am. I don't want to be attacking, but I am. I don't want to run, but I really want to. I want to be accepting of myself and fight for myself as much as I would fight for others, but I am scared and feel weak when it comes to me, and I don't feel the same drive to do so just now.

I do know I can do this, I know I am strong; now I just need to emotionally reconnect with that side of me. It is hard.

He did apologize when I came back in, but I was not ready to hear it and I cried; I don't know why. I feel like I am losing Him.

Peace out.

I AM FEELING OKAY

I am feeling better after talking with you. Understanding that I am not running, but doing the right thing to grow in the right way helps me. I can't worry too much about how He will do this; easy to say, hard to do. My energy today, for the first time, feels like it is coming back. I am concentrating on staying focused on myself and the things I need to work on. I don't want to bog myself down by labeling myself as a failure because I am not doing Real Love exactly right; I am doing the best I can. I know this is going to be super good for me, but uncertain how this feels. I know I need to trust myself and Real Love . . . baby steps.

I am enjoying not feeling overwhelmed over the situation last night with Him. It is freeing not to take and absorb, and to not stuff down. I want to work on having a stronger voice without feeling like I am being a bitch. I am having a hard time accepting this part of my voice, which is not being a bitch, but actually loving myself . . . Sounds weird to me when I read it back. I am feeling okay today.

Peace out

MOTHER'S DAY

*T*oday is much, much, much better! I am feeling better emotionally, just from that little talk we had yesterday. He and I have not really talked since the argument. Last night He did say to me that He was feeling frustrated and not heard at work the day we had the argument and so apologized. I just said, "Okay," and "Thank you." I did not know what to say.

There is something that has been eating at me, and I know it should not bother me, but on Mother's Day He contacted my mom and talked to her and then told me. I did say to Him in the past that if He wanted to talk to her, that was His business. With Him, I don't want to know, because when He tells me that He called my mom or emailed her, I kinda get a knot in my stomach because I am feeling like I am being judged by Him. I get the sense that He is contacting her because I won't. I don't want to, but it's always there, and I am afraid that it will encourage my mom to push further; she is really good at wiggling in and taking over.

I don't know if I should say anything or what. It sounds so mean and unloving. I do not share all the stuff I went through emotionally with Him, because His childhood sucked just as badly, and I do not want to play the "I suffered more than you" game. We were both unheard and discounted. It is not an overwhelming feeling and in the past I just let it fade away, but it has popped up in my thoughts several times this past week and I don't know if I should let it go or what.

The issue is not with my mom, but Him contacting her and then telling me about it briefly. It is weird, because I don't care if anyone else contacts her and talks about her, it just bothers me when He does it. So, I am thinking it is not about the actual action of contacting her, but the emotions it stirs in me; like feeling He is being more concerned with her feelings than mine in the relationship between my mom and me. I am feeling like He doesn't care, or discounts the suffering I experience when I am involved with my mom.

I don't know how to bring it up without feeling like I am trying to control Him, and also fearing that He will tell me I am wrong or that I am too hard on her . . . I just don't know . . . I don't know if that is it.

Peace Out

Don't Know

I am feeling hopeful about my ability to move forward. Tonight my thoughts are traveling to my intimate relationship with Him. I am feeling guilty because I am not responding to him the way I think I should. I don't know how to approach Him. I am kind of confused and I am having a hard time figuring out my true feelings. When I start to think about it I just stop, because I do not want to deal with it at this moment. I do not know if I have the ability to look at this right now. I am now focusing on getting through the next few months of dealing with recovering from cancer. I do not want it to be at the cost of our relationship, and I think that is why I have this fear that He is frustrated with me. I just, at this moment, don't have it in me to worry much about how He is doing. It feels foreign to me, which I am sure feels foreign to Him because of the dynamics within our relationship. I do not know if I should share with Him, as the last time I tried to share my feelings and thoughts it went south really fast. Mmm . . . What to do?

Don't know…

Peace out.

Typical Me

I am still mulling over how I truly feel about myself, my accountability of where I am currently, and my role in creating this lovely beast called *my life.*

I wish I could snap my fingers and be unconditionally loving, but that would defeat the purpose of this journey to grow into myself and find unconditional love within so I can go and share it with others. It would be so nice, but I guess that is running . . . very typical of me.

I have this urge to be totally honest with Him, telling my truth, but I know instinctually that this is not the time to do this with Him. I am already worrying about having the conversation about my mom with Him. On the one hand, I really want to, my choice, but still fearing his reaction. It has to be shared.

I am also fearful that if I start telling Him the truth, I will not be able to stop and I'll verbally dump on Him, and I know He is not the one to do this with. This is scary because in the past when I shared my feelings with my sister (dumping on her; she is very loving toward Him and me), she does not tell me what to do. She just lets me share and cry until I am done, and then tells me I can do this and it is my choice. I have only shared with her on a few occasions because I didn't want her to stress out when I just needed to talk it out with someone. He did not like this so much. I also did not tell Him that my sister was not judging Him, but trying to help me see it from His side (most of the time). So essentially, I ran, acted like a victim, and attacked by omission because I was not truthful about what was shared, and shut Him out which left Him feeling isolated and alone. In that moment, I did not care how He felt because I was too busy being a victim. Then I would feel guilty and over compensate for shutting him out by clinging.

This is so difficult for me because I can see the path I am standing on; the path I want to take. I can see clearly this is where I need to be, and I want to do this, but (there is always a "but") I am so scared that this might tip the scale for Him and me. I know it is his choice to go or not go, and mine to love Him in his choices.

I also have a choice, and I have to live with the consequences of my choices. I have to trust, but there it is again; trust is so hard. I open up, share, get stomped on emotionally, close up, run, live in victimhood, talk myself out of victimhood and go straight to being clingy, and then start the cycle again. I am a hot mess! Damn it this is tuff!!!!!! What the hell is wrong with me?

I have stuffed these emotions down and now they are seeping up. I just hope I have the strength, faith, and trust in myself and others to be able to be accepting of unconditional love and try to practice being aware.

Peace out

JUDGING

*T*hanks for texting me tonight. You must have had a sense I was feeling a little blue. I smiled when I received your text because I knew someone was thinking of me and cared enough to let me know.

So I watched disk 5 of Real Love; the example about judging is what I think struck a chord with me the most. I have such a fear of being judged that I am always trying to be perfect and am my own worse judge. I want to be seen as a beautiful person, no matter if I am not doing anything, or deciding to do everything because I want to. My actions should not be based on what I feel others expect of me.

I am in fear of being judged, and I beat myself up when I catch myself judging others. I feel like I am being unkind, but I seem to judge without thinking about it. Then, I feel like I am a horrible person, and to make myself feel better I try to be extra nice.

This pattern has worn me down . . . I thought I was doing well, but in reality, I wasn't, because I was not being truthful. Judging also allows me to escape from people so I don't have to interact and can go to victimhood. This particular pattern for me is hard. I attack, then run, and then blame . . . it is such a cycle. I am aware of it sometimes and struggle to step out of the cycle, but I know it is a journey; one step at a time.

In the past if I were quick to judge and put myself at a higher place than the other, I would not have to feel the pain as much when I was judged back by that person. If I do it first, I will avoid some or all of the pain I fear might come by being honest and being me. I then do not have to communicate I am wrong, and I get to be right; something I don't like to see in myself, but it is there and I need to see it to accept it and change.

I am trying to avoid being hurt again emotionally. Having someone to share this information with lessens the fear for me; I can stop splashing so much in the pool and realize I can do this; still in the pool, but maybe just wading, building up the courage to take that first step out of the pool and feel safe enough to do it.

Sharon, I really want you to know that you are becoming very important to me. I am not being clingy, I just want you know that I really think you are special.

You are wiggling into my trust zone and I am letting you in, which will allow me to trust you more . . . I know it takes time and I know I can do this . . . it is just wearing trust to comfortably break it in and fully embrace it. I know I can do this...

Thank you for listening ...

Peace Out

DAMN IT!!!

*T*oday was kinda weird for me. I overslept and was really, really late for work. On the way to work I was cut off by a car and I flipped the guy off; so very unlike me! I did it without even thinking about it.

The first reaction in my head was, "Oh . . . I probably upset that person and he was probably having a bad day and did not see me." Then I thought, "That is something my mom would do and did! Damn it!!!" probably because we were speaking about her. Then I let it go, but thought it was weird because I have not done that since I was in my twenties.

I do feel better and lighter having shared all that stuff in a safe way with Him. We did hug for a bit and I told Him thank you for listening and supporting me.

Peace out

DIFFERENT EXPERIENCES

I am just going to share stuff about me to get it out. If you don't respond I am totally fine.

It is one thing to talk about different experiences, and another to commit to writing and sharing. I need to see where it started to

23

understand why I am the way I am . . . to create an understanding . . . to create a change.

Okay here I go...

I grew up with a mentally ill mom (bi-polar). I felt like the target of her rage and frustrations. Wait; I need to back track. I was born a triplet to an eighteen year old mom. My dad was only twenty-one at the time, and left when my mom had an episode either while pregnant with us or shortly after. My mom did not have support . . . She was in a bad place. Of course, I do not remember this, but it is what I was told. My mom gave birth to us and went to a mental hospital . . . and we were left in the hospital to die. We only weighed about seven pounds all together, and we were not supposed to survive. We were in the hospital for several months, and then we were split up when we went home because my mom could not take care of us. I do not remember any of this but from that point on my childhood was a cycle of physical, sexual, and verbal abuse by people in my family. It was my life and I knew no difference until much later. We, meaning the triplets, were discarded and not wanted and we were bounced around for a while until no one wanted us (around the age of four). Then it was back with my mom, and in the summer we would go to my grandparents for a week or so. There was a lot of verbal and physical abuse by mom because she did not know how to cope, and then there was sexual abuse as well. I played protector to my brothers and sister, and also the other kids that came along with the roommates and boyfriends at times. I could not stand watching them get beat and punished with no tenderness or caring, so I would tell my mom that it was my fault. She would do this cycle with my baby brother, because I would always take the blame for him; especially when he was a toddler. I did not mind at the time because it was too much for him and I was able to fade out of the pain and move forward. It is . . . was an escape. My mom would then be okay for a while and life would go on. There was never any consistency; always craziness, never happy. I knew at a young age, maybe by seven or eight, that this stress was not good, and I tried even harder to bring normalcy to our lives by cooking dinner and doing homework with my sister and little brother. My twin brother was just as out of control as my mom at this point, constantly verbally and

24

physically attacking us, including my mom. Of course this created even more stress and tension, and the more there was, the more I pulled back and tried to be calm. I am really good at being the calm person when there is craziness around. I am only focusing on the stuff that happened before I was ten, because the older I got, the angrier my mom got. My twin brother just could not stop being angry, or learn to flow with the energy; sometimes it was okay . . . but mostly not.

The memories I have of my mom when I was younger, was of her constantly chipping away at my soul. I wouldn't let her wear me down for too long; probably why she got so upset with me. I refused to give in to her when I knew inside it would be harmful. I know there were some good times, because my mom has pictures of holidays and trips to the beach and stuff like that. I think for me, there are no good memories because it was not real; it was just an illusion, and we were puppets. It was incredible the lengths she would go to prove a point or make someone feel belittled. Like I remember her pulling me out of my bed in the middle of the night by my hair and dragging me down the stairs because I did not clean the dishes the way she wanted the dishes done. She would become infuriated with us for eating the wrong food at the wrong time. Then she would double her efforts when we were late for school, because she did not want to look bad. I hated being late or sick, because that meant trouble with mom.

The funny thing is, when in the past I tried to talk about what happened, she said that it never did and that I was making up stories to get attention and to make her look bad (but that is a whole other story).

My sister and I begged the state to let us stay in foster care on more than one occasion, just so we would have the chance to have normalcy. That didn't happen, but we were able to convince the state to keep us together in the same foster home; it was a small victory, but it was important. The foster parents we had said we were the best kids they ever had, and that is because we were terrified of breaking the rules, or worse, being sent back . . . which always happened.

I don't have a lot of feeling about my childhood, probably because I was disconnected more than I was connected. As I type, I feel like I am just giving the facts of a story. I will say I did cry when you read my previous email back to me because I could finally hear my voice in a way I can't when I talk or write . . . Kinda weird . . . I am done for now . . .

Peace out

I REMEMBER

I want to let you know that I do not have any anger towards my dad or mom. As I have weaved through therapies, and read books on forgiveness and understanding people and why they do the things they do, I have been at least intellectually connecting the dots and realize that it is usually not about me. This understanding came to me while I was quite young; probably ten or so. I remember standing in the backyard with my sister, hiding from my mom and talking to refocus on something different. I remember this conversation because we came to some conclusions; that what was happening to us was not because of what we were or were not doing and that these people where just messed up. We made a pact never to talk about this, which I broke when I was eighteen (Another story), and if we could survive to eighteen we would be okay. That was my goal from that point on; to survive my childhood, because at the time that was the only option.

I had and still have a very deep passion for trying to understand the choices people make in life. I know it stems from my childhood. The question I always struggled with is, "Why do some people pull themselves together and do well in spite of all the stuff they go through, and some don't?" As I learn more, I understand it is an illusion for most people and they are not really all that happy. I understood that happiness came from within. I think that was a survival tool for me.

I am aware of what is going on around me, and I certainly am not delusional about life. I have had an abundance of opportunities to practice *choosing happiness*. I am not saying that I did not have mental bouts with myself about not feeling deserving. I just have learned to put myself in other people's shoes and try to see it from where they are standing. It changes my whole perspective. I also know that I can relate to most people, but I lack tolerance for those who seem to find the negative no matter the situation. I know this is and has been my struggle

26

when dealing with things that I find trivial, but that is huge for another. I know that these stories are manifestations of deeper hurts, but sounding selfish, I think I get kinda mad because people want me to empathize and fix without any thought to me. Then several years ago I discovered the power of the word *No* . . . it really weeds out those people that were there for the wrong reasons. I did not have a hard time letting go, either. It is much harder with family because I love them so much and I do not want to add to their unhappiness (from their point of view). I do not argue much about happiness being a choice . . . I just do it and leave at that.

Anyway, I wanted to address anger. I did have a lot of anguish in me when I was younger; I'm not feeling sorry for myself, but I understood that I had a hard and long journey ahead of me to get straight in my head, and I felt like I was at a disadvantage and viewed myself as something broken that needed to be fixed; that really made me not like me. If someone remotely even suggests that I am a victim, I get really mad. I don't even know why this makes me so mad. Or, on second thought, it is because I have worked and struggled so long on fixing me, that when I start to feel some self-acceptance, the next thing I am being told is that there is still something broken and not quite good enough; it is so deflating to hear that and to be myself . . . Then I start a cycle of trying to fix myself again, to what I think at the moment, is viewed as broken. Maybe it is not so much anger for me but shame about where I have come from. I am willing to share if asked, but I do not just give those stories to people; it is overwhelming to hear or comprehend if there is not a point of reference to relate to. I already have a small inkling that Real Love is the significant path I will need to take to conquer this struggle within myself. I do not have anger, as much as I just feel tapped out when it comes to emotional attachments to my childhood. I wish no ill will toward anyone, because I know it was not about me . . . but I must deal with the aftermath of the choices made by others when I had no voice as a child. It is a humbling journey and the more I grow, the more I love and the more I share.

It took many, many, years to finally have the courage to break with my mom; I was thirty-six. It was hard because I knew she would not understand why and feel like I was hurting her. It came down to me choosing between being miserable or growing deeper into happiness. I chose happiness. I did not know how to explain this to her so she would understand, so I just stopped. I get this was difficult for her, and I had a lot of guilt around that decision . . . because she felt like I was also abandoning her. I know it is painful but I thought about it and thought about it. The best way to let her go was to mourn her while she was still technically alive. The way I see it is that I was able to escape that chaos and she never did. I never felt close to her, but I know she did the best she could. I do not blame her for being her; it is what it is. I love her in the sense that I would love any other person and I hope that she can find some peace and love, however she defines that . . . to maybe stumble upon inner happiness. I wish her the best.

The past cannot be changed, my experiences cannot be changed. My being . . . now *that* can be changed. It is what drives me and moves me to being passionate and loving. The more I grow into me, the more I feel my inner glow. I can really feel it sometimes but I am very private about it. You are the first I ever told because I think you will get it...

Peace out

KINDA STUCK

I don't know if I should talk about my mom; I guess there is some pain when thinking about the actual events, and seeing them in my mind's eye and the pain of being triggered. I still feel separated from those events, but the suffering (emotions) I can relate to no matter whose story it is.

I think it comes down to what we talked about; me feeling judged harshly when I was trying my best. I don't understand how people can inflict pain on another person intentionally; it boggles my mind . . . well, not so much anymore, but it bothers me.

What is even more amazing to me is that I am beginning to have an understanding on a different level concerning the pain I am willing to hold onto to protect others and myself. I understand that it is damaging, but sometimes the fight to be heard is so hard for me because I just take the first sign of being judged as non-approval, so I just stop; I've convinced myself that I am not worth fighting for, and so just give in, which is a big fat lie.

So, I am kinda stuck because I am not sure how to go about trying to be truthful when I need to the most. I can do it when it is not something that triggers me . . . that is the easy part. The part where I need to be strong is where I am lacking. The question is when to fight or not fight for myself . . . especially since I know myself the best.

Do I have to fight or prove myself?

That is where I need my strength, to know that I do not have to prove myself to anyone anywhere. I need to see myself and take responsibility for my choices, and face the consequences of my choices.

The consequences of choices are sometimes something I would have never thought of in a million years, but that is the risk I take when making a choice; that is living. The real issue is not to question my choices when someone else does.

It is removing the biggest obstacles for me; fear and trusting others will be my biggest challenges, but it has to be done . . . one step at a time in order to feel unconditional love. I am starting to feel it here and there when I am open to it; it feels good and encourages me to move forward. I am beginning to take bigger steps and one day I will be able to go right through the emotions and find the peace and joy radiating from within on a consistent basis. I am also realistic in knowing that the radiance will ebb and flow, but it will be recognizable to me now which will and does give me the courage to do what I must to be who I have always naturally wanted to be.

That is it for now…

Love

ANGRY

*W*hen I think of my mom, I have mixed emotions. I know she is dealing with a mental illness which she has decided not to have treated because she believes she was misdiagnosed. Whatever! I am angry because this is her excuse for her bad behaviors. She is always stating that she does not need help with her illness, but then uses it as an excuse when she gets into trouble. She is really good at using legal and mental institutions to get what she wants. There seems to be no help unless she commits an act of violence and is caught while doing it; otherwise, it does not count. I do not want to deal with it and I won't. I am angry because I can see that she is hurting on one side, but defiant on the other side, and because of her ability to manipulate, she was able to hurt me both emotionally and physically. She says she loves me, and then in the next breathe attacks me . . . I am angry that I do not have a close mom/daughter relationship . . . and hoping when I married, that I would finally have that . . . with my mother-in-law. Childish expectations . . . My mother-in-law was openly angry and bitter at the world . . . With my mom it was like living in the land of crazy . . . I never knew how she was going to show up. On the other hand, with my-mother-in-law . . . there was no guessing . . . she was just plain angry all the time . . .

My anger stems from not being able to change those relationships . . . it was not meant to be . . . I understand that my mom will never be "my mom" . . . she does not have it in her . . . she is running scared . . . she will be that way until she dies . . . And that is just sad to think about...

I feel angry, then happy, because I know I don't have to interact with my mom anymore. The pain I feel when looking back is for the girl in me . . . struggling so hard to survive and wanting to be loved . . . and trying to be everything everybody wanted her to be . . . so she could feel seen...

I want to find the reasons through my stories why I am not loveable to my mom . . . because the little girl inside of me knew it was not true . . . she would not believe that she was not loveable . . . but what she did believe, and even sometimes still does today, is that she is not quite as *good* as others...

I knew I was a good girl, I knew instinctively that I was loveable, and I knew I could survive this . . . These beliefs came to be because of sharing with my sister . . . she truly loves me. When my mom would attack me . . . we would talk and she would laugh and say that it wasn't true . . . and I believed her . . . It felt like we were in a battle; us against them . . . it was a test of endurance as to how much crap we could take . .

. I would not break, but I did bend to keep the peace . . . picked my battles . . . with my mom...

One time she actually drove 40 minutes because she was so mad at me for hanging up on her . . . she had called and talked to my brother and sister and both were crying . . . I took the phone . . . I was so angry . . . she had dumped us off at some lady's house and was gone for several days . . . to be with her boyfriend, and we were all sick . . . I asked her who she thought she was. And stated that she was a horrible mother . . . and then slammed the phone down . . . mistake!!! She was there within the hour . . . stomped into where I was sitting . . . lifted my head up and suckered punched me in the face . . . and told me to never disrespect her again . . . then turned around and went back to her boyfriend's house. Needless to say, this was normal stuff for me, but not for the lady we were staying with . . . she was scared and she asked us to leave . . . I get it . . . she had an out . . . It was a mess. It should not have happened, and I still get angry at my mom when I think about that particular incident. That happened not because she was mentally unstable; that happened because she felt inconvenienced and was straight out being a bitch and being especially selfish.

Love

DONE, DONE, DONE

J am still so very angry. I mean, I do not know how to respond to it. I just want to attack Him and hurt Him . . . but I won't. I also understand that this is not just about yesterday. I am mad at Him for apologizing.

He apologized for making me cry. Not about His controlling behavior, not for brow beating me into silence, not for anything. I just get tired of Him acting out and then apologizing, and I am supposed to let it go because He is working on Himself.

I am having a hard time seeing past His selfish behaviors. My feelings at this moment are that He puts himself first and so do I.

My choice, so I live with the consequences. He has said in the past that if I don't like it, I can leave. I don't fully trust His attention because He has

31

talked of divorcing me and how we can do it peacefully. That was right before we started talking with you; but really . . .

I was ready to just say, "Fine, let's do this." So, I find it very confusing when I am told that He is worried about me dying or leaving. Really? It does not feel that way.

I know it is scary to hear about and to watch me deal with this cancer, but I feel like my time to deal with it has passed. He is watching me and I am living it but He knows I am not going to die from cancer; the Doctor even said so . . . at least not thyroid cancer. I am just done, done, done. I am sick of being told that I am not good enough when I know I am. I am so frustrated about being an afterthought. I am trying not to jeopardize what we are trying to do, but my anger toward Him has me in a tizzy. I don't know what to say without sounding like I am attacking.

I am so tired of always having to fight to be seen or heard or loved that I just give up. I do not want to have to earn love from Him, and that is how it feels. He is right and I am wrong.

If I speak up, I am defiant or manipulative. I am not accepted as I am. I am always being pushed to do more and more; it feels lopsided, even if I do it kicking and screaming. I have such a fear of being attacked that I can't fight for myself; anybody else I can fight for, but not me. I just don't know . . . I am rambling and I am so confused.

I know you want me to call people, but I am holding on by a string and am struggling to just reach out to you. I just can't speak to people I don't know. Love has never been unconditional for me, so I am having a hard time trusting complete strangers with my truths.

As I said, I feel like I am betraying Him for even discussing this because I did not ask Him if I could share this, or if He was willing to be seen in this light. It is exposing Him and making Him vulnerable. I feel like I am pushing Him, but I am just trying to be helped. I hope he understands that I am not trying to *expose* him, but rather working on me, which includes Him.

I know that I am irrational at times, but I also know it stems from fear. I just want to run . . . I am hanging on to the edge of the cliff and I am losing my grip.

COMMITTED

I have given much thought to our last conversation and committing to Real Love at the level needed.

In short:

I cannot give.

I am not committed to making three calls a day.

I am not committed to going to group twice a week.

I am committed to journaling with you, if you allow me to continue.

I am committed to meeting with you (last three sessions) if you want to.

I am committed to meeting new people in Real Love outside of group and connecting that way.

I am committed to calling someone when I feel empty, afraid, mad, etc.

I am committed to studying Real Love and continually practicing what I am learning.

I am committed to the consequences of my choices made.

I want to be able to focus on our relationship in a positive manner.

I need to stay focused on my health, both physically and mentally.

At this time, I am doing the best I can and I cannot add much more to my plate.

I understand that some of my ups and downs have to do with the balancing of my hormones, and I need to be accepting of that and be able to be okay with being confused and unable to be clear on what is or is not okay with me.

With Love

COOKING

I talked to Him and told Him that I will no longer be cooking. He asked, "Was it because I had one bad day?" I said, "No, I just do not like to cook." He simply said, "Okay." He asked me how our appointment went. I told Him that Real Love will be the best thing we ever commit to, that it will bring us together or tear us apart; our choice. I don't know if that is what I should have said, but it was not said emotionally, just matter-of-factly. He just looked at me. I left it at that. I am feeling surer of myself, and the stronger I feel, the less I walk in fear. It is a hard process and I feel like this is the biggest challenge I have purposely put in my path. Untangling is a feeling of just relief and not having to be concerned about guarding myself so much. My anger is tempered and manageable (not reacting or attacking). Not that I don't screw up, but at least I can recognize, call, get loved, move forward. I guess being knocked to my knees needs to happen to get my attention; I am determined not to be distracted.

With love

THANK YOU

S haron, you keep drifting into my thoughts so I will share with you.

I do not know why I keep reflecting on you, but there must be something there that I have not been able to wiggle out yet.

This is where my mind keeps wandering, and usually I would not share my feelings but I am feeling prompted do so.

You are such a lovely person, and I feel the urge to tell you that . . . for no other reason than I feel compelled to tell you.

I place you in high regard, and view you as a person with integrity, who has the experience of creating a feeling of being nurtured, who has the ability to connect with people, and as someone who is accepting.

Thank you for being committed, believing in me, being accessible, giving with no strings attached, defining opportunities to grow, and lifting me to a higher self-awareness.

34

I wanted to let you know that your kindness and love toward me has influenced my life and my understanding of others. Your acceptance of me, as I am, with no expectations, has had the ripple effect of me practicing and emulating the gift of acceptance and love toward others.

There is nothing more humbling then to have someone like you give unconditionally and pour so much love, faith, and belief into me to help me not feel empty.

Thank you does not seem like enough to express the gratitude I have for your gift of being you, and for seeing me for who I am.

You truly inspire me to be a better version of me, and in this moment I have happiness and joy in knowing that I am unconditionally loved by you and me; it centers me. I am smiling

With love

PEACE IN THE MOMENT

First of all, I really enjoyed your presentation; it just reinforced what I believe to be true. I like being around people who care, and don't ask anything of me. I am trying to stay focused, as I am currently in the process of getting my body prepared for the next step in beating this cancer. This is more mentally draining for me than physically. I am trying not to get caught up in the fear of not knowing how my body will react to the treatment, and to be at peace in the moment and to be grateful for all that I have and am. This can be difficult when so much is being asked of me on a mental level, and trying to explain the need to not do anything is hard when it is a one-sided conversation.

I have been thinking a lot about Him. I love Him so much and it is hard to fight the urge not to run to do things or say things to make him feel happy. I know in the long run this is counterproductive, and only puts a Band-Aid on the situation. I will say it is easier sometimes to just give imitation love to Him because that is what he is looking for in moments of behaviors; I really struggle with that. I really feel the need to be selfish right now when it comes to Him. The downside is that the more I speak, the more resistant He is. I have come to realize that He does not want to talk about my feelings; He wants me to agree with Him. Sharing my personal thoughts with Him about my struggles seems like something He does not want to hear about or deal with, so I do not share that with Him much unless he asks a specific question. I see that it causes Him so much stress, and that is the last thing I want to do because I know who He is and where He came from. He wants to be loved unconditionally, and He is, because we love Him so much . . . but he can't feel our love and acceptance. That really kinda makes me feel sad when I think about it. I cannot do anything to change that. He has to be the one to decide when those walls come down.

I am in a quandary about things at the moment because I am limited to what I can do right now and for the next few months. I just need to focus on being healthy both mentally and physically. I am not sure how this will work out with my family, and I am trying to untangle at a steady pace so they do not go into shock. No matter what is said, I do not think that I am being selfish, but proactive in finding my happiness and inner joy. I really do like being with myself and exploring and learning and loving others. It is what brings me inner joy.

Also,

I have always thought forgiveness was a selfish act, but in a good way. I view forgiveness as an act of love toward self, as it releases you from the bonds of the act that needed forgiveness. The other party is accountable for his or her part.

Sharon, I do feel your love and I so much appreciate it. It helps me to feel safe and have the courage I need to speak my truth. It is such a process. I do trust you and know that you love me. It makes my heart glow.

Much love

TREATMENT

I wanted to let you know that I am off my meds for treatment and will be dealing with the effects of that for the next week or so. Starting Saturday, I will be at the hospital daily for injections, then in-

36

house for radiation treatment. While I am in-house at the hospital, I will have limited access to email and phone. Not exactly sure how this is all going to go down. I will email periodically, but wanted to let you know I am not pulling away and I am bringing my Real Love books and CD's with me so I can stay focused in Real Love. I am going to journal just to get my feelings out as well. It seems to help me. I am trying to work the remainder of this week, and then taking the next week off, and possibly the following week after that. I am going to get clarification on my questions when I go to the hospital, to make sure I am mentally prepared for the next few weeks. You are in my thoughts.

Love

NEEDING TO LEAN IN

I was thinking about what we discussed last night on the phone. I have some fear around moving forward because of dealing with Him.

I do not know how to handle myself because one minute we are communicating and the next either He shuts down or I do. I see the purpose and the absolute need to *lean in* to the Real Love community. I will push through my doubts and fears and do what I need to do to feel love from other people besides Him. I have difficulty watching the back and forth of His emotions regarding Real Love and I find myself agreeing and supporting those feelings. But when I stop and listen to myself, I do not agree, and understand that I was just agreeing and lying to "keep the peace." It's another form of running. I want to keep the balance . . . but then I show imitation love . . . towards myself and others. I am taking this one day at a time but need to get this out of me . . . expressing myself just makes me feel complete. I also try not to think too far ahead because at the end of the day, I absolutely know, deep down inside, that I will need to be strong and face his emotional meltdown no matter what I choose . . . it seems this will be inevitable. I hope that the emotional meltdown will be a positive step for Him. I know I am not responsible for His choices or consequences, I just don't know if I have the courage to watch and not step in to try and *fix* Him . . . This is one of my biggest fears. This is why I need to *Lean In*...

That is what I am thinking about for a while…

Love

ONE OF THOSE DAYS

*H*ave you ever had days that are for the most part wonderful, but have challenges? Yesterday I had one of those days. I was late to work . . . oh well. I could not find the doctor's office after driving for hour and a half. When I did find it, I was having difficulty containing my emotions. I really needed to speak with the doctor, and was upset because I called the office and told them I was having trouble finding the office. The lady on the phone said if I was more than 10 minutes late I could not be seen that day; I was 15 minutes late. Being that I drove around for what seemed like forever, I was in tears by the time I found the office, but was trying to pull myself together. This is where I wanted to stop the world to get off and just breakdown. Instead, I walked into the office with tears in my eyes (I could not hold back), and asked if I could have a copy of my test results to take to the hospital. No can do, doctor has to sign off on release of reports and is currently doing a biopsy. So I took a deep breath, and asked if I could wait for the doctor to complete his biopsy and have two minutes of his time. She would check. I asked for a moment to go outside and make a call. I dialed the number and the person was not available. I was beginning to become overwhelmed, so I took another breath and dialed Him. My daughter answered. Dang; she was so happy to hear from me . . . I could hear it in her voice. I politely asked to talk to Dad. Those few words revealed my emotions, and she replied, "What is wrong?" I didn't answer for a moment . . . she then asked, "You want to talk to Dad?" I just shook my head yes, because I could not even say the word without crumbling on the phone, but I finally squeaked it out. Whew, now on to Him . . . I just blurted out, "I am having a really bad moment." Then He said something I don't remember, but when He stopped talking, I said, "Just let me tell you what I am dealing with currently so I can go back and deal with the doctor's office." Then He said something, and then I rambled for three or four minutes . . . by the time I was done, I felt better, but I did have a twinge of guilt for dumping on Him. I let it go, because in that moment I had

38

needed to release my feelings so I could be gracious and loving enough to deal with the doctor and staff. I told Him thank you for letting me talk my emotions out, and told Him I had to go and I would see Him later...

I went back inside much calmer, waited a while, and saw the doctor. He said he did not know I was being scheduled for my radiation treatment. I do remember the hospital calling me to tell me that they were unable to get a hold of my doctor, so went to another doctor to okay the procedure; the doctor who did the actual surgery. This news did not sit well with the doctor I was dealing with in the moment. Anyway, I asked what he thought, and ultimately he said it was up to me. I have decided to move forward with my treatment and I told him that. I want to get beyond this hurdle. He said okay, but that I'd need to have several more tests done. I said okay.

That was my day (Friday) in a nutshell.

I am not sure how I am feeling other than overwhelmed about parts of my day, but not my whole day. I am doing a lot of inner evaluating. I am struggling to hear my own voice right now. I have to stop and really think about what I need and want, and that is hard for me to do. I will do this though. I know I can...

P.S. I had my first injection today, but you probably knew that already.

Wanted to share...

Love

"How Are You Doing?"

$\mathcal{I}$ almost cried when I read your question, "How are you doing?" I am not really asked that very often. I am a jumbling mess of emotions, and I am scared of the physical and hormonal downward spiral I am on. I am not sure if it is a good thing or not, because I seem to very weepy over the smallest things, and feel the need to go inside and just mentally hold myself.

Last night, at about one in the morning, I had this overwhelming need to have someone hold me. I did not know what to do because I have not allowed myself to feel that openly. I wanted, so badly, to be held. The only thing I could think of to do was to go to my computer and read some of your past responses . . . it helped. I then wanted to get my mind off of it so I could go back to sleep, so I picked up a book. Then I read this passage in the book, *The Shack* -- (Papa talking to Mack) *"Honey, there is no easy answer that will take your pain away. Believe me, if I had one, I used it now. I have no magic wand over you to make it all better. Life takes a bit of time and a lot of relationship."* I cried when I read that because as much as I don't want to feel the pain, I must see it, acknowledge it, and release it through love. Then I read when Saraya was speaking with Mack -- *"You cannot produce trust, just like you cannot "do" humility. It either is or isn't. Trust is the fruit of a relationship in which you know you are loved."*

Crying again . . . That is why I need Real Love. There are only two options with Love: have it or don't. So much to think about . . . I really wish I was there to have you physically hold me and feel safe in doing that, with no expectations. I trust you immensely and truly love you. Yesterday, when He started talking about your session and Real Love, I just listened and then responded, "I trust Sharon immensely and truly love her." I think He was a little perplexed because I did not agree or ask questions . . . I just left it at that and that was the end of that discussion. I told the truth and it felt good.

Gotta go off to the hospital for another injection!

Loving and thinking of you

THE BOOK

S o, at the hospital I picked up a book, got through about a page, and started crying . . . I was reading a chapter in The Garden about people's feelings about rights . . . and control. People at the hospital were walking by and just staring at me as I cried and tried to read this book. I could not get past this page . . . I just reread it and reread it, crying the whole time, not really caring who saw me crying . . . Can you believe that?! ME, not caring how people were taking my emotions . . . Is that selfish? Mmm, doesn't matter . . . I needed to absorb that information.

This book is bombing the hell out of my emotional wall into bits and pieces.

While this was going on, Toni from Real Love texted me and asked how I was feeling today. Oh dang! I immediately thought about what I had said this morning to you in my email about no one really asking me how I was doing . . . and then in one day, two people asked. It made me think about not having expectations . . . meaning, instead of assuming someone in my family would naturally ask me that question, it can come from another source. Then I realized I did not care where or who; just knowing that I am thought of and loved made a shift in me. Then Toni and I texted back and forth a little and she said something that made me stop in my tracks; that everybody in that group on Wednesday is thinking about me and loving me. I know you have told me this at least a couple of hundred times by now, but I was not feeling it because it was too ambiguous for me. Then I thought, *I know that . . . why am I just being so selective in who I contact? There were only eight of us and it was indeed an intimate evening in our sharing. I did feel connected and loved, even if I doubted my ability to communicate without rambling. Several people had handed me their phone numbers besides Toni . . .*

So I got in my car at the hospital and before driving home, I texted another person; Sheri, who was in my Wednesday group. I just let her know that she had stumbled into my thoughts, courtesy of Toni, and that I wanted to connect with her. She also responded, and I was so . . . I don't know how to express accurately, but I guess the word would be . . . loved. To walk through fear and get over my fear of rejection is hard. I just want to be loved and accepted for who I am, and not have fear in showing ME. I am actually quite a lovely person and I do enjoy my own company. I also really like being me. I am *seeing* more and more of me and not holding to the fear so much, because I have the RL community to lean in to . . . my circle of trust is growing . . . ever so slowly, but still growing . . . and that is a good thing . . . . *Love you*

LITTLE GIRL

Okay, I am going to share with you what my world is like on the inside a little. I hope it makes sense when you read it, and know that I am sharing

41

from a place of love. I will need to speak in the 3rd person to share with you.

I really am trusting that this not too weird for you. I never, ever want to take away from your heart song; only add to your heart song when possible.

I know I don't have to say it, but thank you for showing us your tenderness; it is a most precious gift to share . . . and my heart swells with love for you for trusting us enough to share that piece of you with us.

Breathe . . .

Wednesday group:

J (the woman in me) cried when I pulled up to the meeting because I knew it was time to show Little Girl that not only was she loved by me, Sharon, and Papa (Spirit), but that everybody finds her precious and wants to hear (feel) her heart song (love), just as much as Mom (me) and Papa (Spirit) does; it is so beautiful. That Mom (the woman in me), wanted her to come and see how pretty the world can be. And that Mom knew how very scared Little Girl was, but promised to be with her the whole time . . . and that she didn't have to say anything if she did not feel safe enough, and just being there was enough for now if that is all she could do.

Little Girl was so curious and happy about what Mom wanted to share, because she liked best the stories with Sharon in them. She wanted to go, but as she got to the door she became very frightened. She started shaking her head no because she did not want to go through the door; it meant having to feel deep pain and she did not want to go. Mom embraced her and whispered to her what Sharon had told her, that she loves us and wants to see you and this is the only way; through the darkness.

Little Girl wanted to see Sharon so, so much. Mom asked, "Can you feel that, little one?" Little Girl stopped being scared long enough to stand with Mom. Mom asked again, lovingly, "Do you feel it, little one?" She looked straight into Mom's eyes and saw the love shining and swirling around them, and coming to rest around them, so she shook her head yes. Mom asked, "Do you know what you are feeling, sweet one?"

Little Girl just stared back at Mom holding her hand now. Mom looked back into Little Girl's eyes, "Sweet one, that is Sharon and Papa (spirit). Feel how much they love you, dear one . . . you are wanted." Little Girl's eyes began to grow as she became aware of Sharon's and Papa's (spirit) heart songs. Little Girl's heart was beaming, and she so much wanted to share her heart song with Sharon too. Little Girl remembered that Mom and Papa (spirit) loved it when she shared her heart song with them.

Little Girl looked at Mom and fear flashed across her face as she asked, "Do I have to tell Sharon my heart secret to share my heart song? Does she really, really, love us?" She looked down and stared at her baby toes . . . "Will Sharon be mad at me?" Mom went to her knees; she saw how scared she truly was, and whispered to her, "Dear sweet one, you have to share your whole heart. Sharon loves us so, so much and she will never, ever hurt you; even if you thought you were taking away from her heart song. She loves us deeply." Little Girl looked into Mom's eyes and said, "What if Sharon doesn't want to hear my heart song?" Mom looked at Little Girl tenderly, "Oh, sweet little one, Sharon wants to see you just as much as you want to see her." Little Girl knew Mom never lies to her, so she believed her completely.

Little Girl looked at Mom, still embraced lightly in her arms, and said, "Look what I have." Mom looked into Little Girl's hands and just smiled, because she already knew what Little Girl was holding. Little Girl exclaimed, "I have been carrying this with me, close to my heart. Can I always keep it there?" Mom smiled at Little Girl and said, "That is such a precious gift, little one. Sharon will be so happy to know that her tenderness is so close to our heart." Little Girl looked straight into Mom's eyes and asked, "Do I have to ever give it back?" Mom smiled and answered, "Sharon gave that to us to have forever and ever." Little Girl didn't say anything, and looked at her gift in wonderment . . . gently closing her eyes for a moment . . . she then looked at Mom and said, "I am ready, Mom." Mom stood up and just above a whisper said, "I am here, and I love you to the moon and back, little one."

As I came back to the room, I heard, "Barbara, did you want to share?"

I shifted and said something . . . I am not sure what . . . Then I was asked in the midst of my rambling, "What age were you when the pain started?" I stopped, a little stunned by the question, and closed my eyes . . . and looked at Little One . . . and said, "It is time, sweetness..." Little Girl stepped forward and looked . . . that was enough; I collapsed my emotional walls so sweet Little Girl could be seen, heard, loved, and feel safe enough to share.

I was blubbering and pouring my heart out and I couldn't look at anybody. The group was so gentle with my tenderness, because I felt like a three year old . . . and I was fully out as a three year old girl. You know how when a three year old is so exhausted that all they can do is cry for attention?

That is me.

I LOVE YOU TO THE MOON AND BACK

When I woke up, Little Girl was waiting patiently for Mom. She knew she was very weak from being so sick. Little Girl could not hold back, but she didn't want to say it to Mom too loudly, because Mom was so happy that Little Girl felt Sharon's love when they had to do the first scan, because Mom was so, so, very sick . . . but she couldn't hold it back. "I am so scared that I can't do the scan again. I don't want to go." Mom just looked into her face and said, "We have to, little one . . . Mom needs you to be brave for just a little longer."

"Okay, I can be brave for a little longer. I can do that for you, Mom." Little Girl whispered . . . she knew if Mom could protect her, she would. Mom looked into her scared little face, and spoke softly, "Little One, look at me, sweetheart." Little Girl hesitated, then looked into Mom's eyes and Mom looked back into Little Girl's eyes and said, "I love you to the moon and back, little one." Little Girl still felt scared but she knew in her heart that Mom never lies to her and that she loves her from the moon back, really, really. She felt brave again.

Little Girl was not so sure she felt very brave at all. She silently just sat there and looked at Mom and got scared again. Little Girl wanted to cry, but Mom could not hold her just then, so she asked Mom instead, "Can we ask Sharon if she loves us? She said we had to ask." Mom picked up the phone and texted to Sharon, *I am feeling so very weak . . . this is so much, Sharon. Please whisper to me that you love me and that you're holding me. I have to be brave again today. I love you deeply.* Mom set the phone down and could see that Little Girl was so very anxious for Sharon to respond . . . and she waited, not too long, but to Little Girl it felt like a forever wait because she wanted to believe . . . Mom said to Little Girl, "Be patient, little one . . . she will answer. I promise..."And Mom picked up the phone to look, just to reassure Little Girl, and Mom smiled and read, *Love you dear one.* Little Girl was soooo surprised she answered, and she asked Mom if she could text one more thing to Sharon . . . Mom hesitated, and felt Little Girl needing to text just one more thing . . . So Mom texted Sharon back, *Loving you, I am scared.* This time, Little Girl was not quite so anxious . . . she knew Sharon would answer as soon as she could. Mom smiled at Little Girl because she knew how hard it was for her to be patient . . . but she was . . . and Sharon did text back, *I Love you.*

Little Girl felt brave again.

Mom could not sleep . . . she tried, but little Girl kept forgetting that Sharon loved her. Mom could not ignore Little Girl anymore . . . she was still scared and was not sure she could be brave. Mom looked at Little Girl and asked, "Would you like to share a story about one of your heart songs with Sharon, Little One?" Little Girl loved sharing her heart songs with Mom and Papa (spirit) and she really, really wanted to share another one with Sharon. Little Girl told Sharon one just last night, and she was trying to be patient because she knew Sharon would be so very happy when she got her first story about her heart song from her . . . but Little Girl was scared. Mom looked at Little Girl and saw that Little Girl was scared. Mom asked, "What is wrong, Little One?" Little Girl tipped down her head and barely could muster a whisper, "My first story of my heart song was especially for Sharon." And Little Girl wanted with all her heart for Sharon to love her first heart song to her. Mom just smiled at Little Girl and said, "Sharon will love all the stories of your heart song. Are you ready to tell Sharon another story from your heart song now?" Little Girl just smiled at Mom and Mom wrote Little Girl's story of her heart song for her. Little Girl was so happy.

Little Girl was becoming restless as the story of her heart song came to the end. She really had to be brave right now . . . but she wasn't. Little Girl asked Mom to tell Sharon she was scared. Mom texted Sharon, OMG . . . *I am having such anxiety today about doing these scans, probably because I'm feeling so weak. I am minutes away from doing the scan.* Then Mom was put into the scanner.

Mom could feel how scared Little Girl was . . . she could not stop panicking. Mom kept saying, "Keep your eyes closed for me, little one," but Little Girl barely heard her . . . The fear was distracting Little Girl because she could hear a person talking on the phone, and the table was making funny sounds, and Mom felt very weak. Mom tried to get Little Girl's attention back, but it was too late . . . she opened her eyes . . . and screamed and ran behind Mom to feel safe again.

Mom asked to be let out of the scanner for a moment to collect herself and gather her thoughts. She closed her eyes and took deep breathes . . . this always calmed Little Girl. Mom opened her eyes and said, "I can continue." The nurse replied, "We have to start the scan over. It cannot be paused." Little Girl, behind Mom, froze, and just kept saying, "I am so sorry, Mom." Mom replied, "Come here, little one. I forgot to hold you. It is not your fault." Mom embraced Little Girl heart-to- heart, and whispered, "Ready?" Mom could feel Little Girl relax in her arms. "Close your eyes honey . . . can you feel my heart song?" Little Girl melted into Mom and closed her eyes.

Mom was weak and she needed help with Little Girl because she knew she could not keep Little Girl calm if she got distracted again; Mom just did not have the strength to hold Little Girl for so long. Mom kept her eyes closed and opened her heart further and asked for Papa's (spirit) and Sharon's heart songs to help hold little one . . . she asked again . . . And then, little by little, Mom and Little Girl felt Papa's (spirit) and Sharon's heart songs and they both drifted into the song.

"Barbara, the scan is done. You can leave now," the nurse said. Mom stood up and Little Girl immediately chimed in, "I am sorry, Mom, truly. I want to tell Sharon what happened." So Mom found her phone and looked, and read, *Love you.* Mom paused for a moment and texted back, *I didn't do so well. I opened my eyes . . . Then little Girl screamed.* Sharon was right there and texted back, *You forgot I love you.* Mom looked at little Girl and paused . . . and collected her thoughts . . . and she agreed with Sharon, and looked at Little Girl and said, "We both forgot Sharon loves us." Little Girl didn't know what to say . . . so she just looked up at Mom . . . and said, "Do you think she is mad at us?" Mom said, "No," and texted Sharon back, *Just for a moment. I had to start over and Little Girl closed her eyes and listened for Sharon's heart song . . . Then she settled down and she heard it.*

Sharon just replied, *Good.*

For some reason that reply, *Good,* scared Little Girl. Mom was too tired to pay much attention, so they got in the car and drove. Mom couldn't stop feeling how sad Little Girl felt because she thought she did something wrong. Mom could not endure watching Little Girl with her head bowed and feeling all alone. Mom took out her phone again and did not know if Sharon would understand what she was going to text and how much it meant to Little Girl . . . it didn't matter . . . Little Girl did not want Mom, she wanted Sharon. So Mom typed, *Sharon, Little Girl needs to hear you say you love her from the moon and back...*

Sharon replied, *Love you from the moon and back.*

Mom was so relieved that Sharon responded so quickly so she could show Little Girl . . . and she did.

Little Girl, with tears in her eyes, asked Mom to type back to Sharon, *"I love you to the moon and back, Sharon,"* and she felt very loved.

DARKNESS

I hope you don't mind me sharing in the 3rd person . . . I will address that when I can get out what I want to share, and it is difficult to do in 1st person. I just want you to see me . . . I love you . . .

47

om (woman in me) knew this conversation with Him was going somewhere intense. Mom pushed Little Girl behind her to protect her as much as possible, but could not say anything to her just yet. He was not being angry, He wasn't yelling and screaming, but being morose . . . and that is when he was the scariest to us. Mom looked straight into Little Girl's eyes and Little Girl just knew, with no words, that she needed to run so Mom could protect her. Little Girl was so scared, and didn't want to see the darkness, but before she got too far away she heard what He said to Mom and Little Girl felt Mom being stunned into silence, and the darkness starting to spread over Mom.

Little Girl ran and ran, away from Him and Mom . . . she could not turn back, she was too afraid of the dark, and she knew Mom was being enfolded into the darkness . . . tears started pouring down Little Girl's face. She couldn't see Mom, but she could feel her sadness and hear her weeping as she ran to the furthest part of her heart so as not to see the darkness . . . the darkness began to embrace her fully, and Little Girl felt the pain so intensely . . . and was so very scared that Mom's heart song was dying and that she would be truly alone. Little Girl, wide-eyed with fear, heard Mom repeat what He said, trying to be brave, "I have never been in love with you but I love you." Mom only heard, "I don't love you." Little Girl only heard, "I don't want you." Little Girl never, ever wanted to see Him again.

Mom was stunned to silence. She just sat there and closed her eyes and worried. Mom could not find Little Girl and she became very mad at Him for scaring her. Mom thought He was so mean to be untender with Little Girl's heart song. She was upset too . . . at the thoughtlessness and the disregard He had for them. She knew in that moment that to save Little Girl, she could not try to help save Him, and that made Mom's sorrow deepen more than she ever thought possible. She wept and wept because she felt the divide beginning and she could not stop it . . . and she wept . . . and breathed . . . then gathered herself and went to find Little Girl . . . because Mom felt how very, very scared she was . . . it was so overpowering.

Mom could not find Little Girl, and she was worried. So she just started talking to her because Mom knew Little Girl could hear her. "Sweetheart, it's okay, we are done now. He is not here anymore (our heart). I am sorry I scared you and I could not protect you and the Loved Ones (my children) from the darkness like I said I would. I promise to try my best not to let the darkness in anymore. Come see what I have for you." Mom tried to refocus on what Little Girl cherished most. It took a moment. because Mom realized she had almost lost it; her heart song . . . it was so very small, but she could share what she had with Little Girl and the Loved Ones . . . to bring her out, so she could hold her and let her know that no matter what, Mom loved her from the moon and back.

Mom searched for several days and was growing sadder and sadder because Little Girl was too scared to come and share. Mom became so angry with Him, and Little Girl felt that too, and it scared her. And Mom waited and waited . . . and the anger started to unravel . . . and Mom so badly wanted to see Little Girl again. Mom whispered to Little Girl's heart, "I am here sweetheart. I am not mad anymore. I want to hold you..." and Little Girl knew that Mom never lies to her, so she took one step out of the deepest part of the darkness . . . And she stood there until Mom could see her. Little Girl was so scared that Mom could not see her . . . she waited . . . Then Mom saw her, and she cried as she embraced Little Girl . . . and Mom just whispered over and over, "I am so sorry, I am so sorry." Little Girl whispered into Mom's ear, "Mom, I love you to the moon and back too." Mom cried harder and just held Little Girl until the darkness started to fade away a little bit. Little Girl took Mom's face into her hands and looked into Mom's eyes and said, "Did you lose your heart song?" Mom answered, "Baby Girl, no one can ever lose their heart song; sometimes people just have a hard time finding and hearing (feeling) their heart song and sharing. They are scared too. My heart song is very tender, but I want to share it with you and the Loved Ones." Little Girl smiled into Mom's eyes and she felt safe again.

THE QUESTION

ittle Girl knew Mom had spoken to Sharon today on the phone. She could hear them talking, and she was so excited that Mom could talk

49

to her so she would not feel so weak anymore. When Mom hung up, she sat in the car and thought about what Sharon had said. Little Girl should share her heart songs with everyone. Little Girl had heard Mom quickly reply to Sharon that she has called some people, and also texted, but that Little Girl knew that Mom was afraid to share Little Girl's heart songs with anyone else but Sharon and Papa (Spirit).

As Mom walked into the hospital, Little Girl was sooooo excited, because Sharon wanted to share her heart songs with others. Mom was worried and didn't know quite how to tell Little Girl what Sharon had said. Mom did not pay much attention to Little Girl when she was joyful and dancing. Mom always would just watch Little Girl dance and move to her heart song, but Mom never, ever danced with Little Girl to their heart songs heart to heart, because she was afraid someone would see.

Mom sat watching Little Girl dance with joy while she thought about Sharon. Mom could see how much joy Sharon's heart song brought Little Girl, and she never wanted to take her precious gift away . . . even unintentionally. Mom started to think and think, and asked herself, "How can I get Little Girl to come share her heart songs with others?" Mom already knew that she was going to Sharon's group on Sunday, so she thought about that for a moment. Sharon told Mom that it would be safe . . . then Mom thought about the Wednesday group meeting when Little Girl had cried and cried but felt so much love when she finally was able to calm herself down.

Then suddenly, an idea came to Mom, but she had to ask Sharon first. She was a little hesitant because she was not sure if Sharon wanted to do this, so she thought some more . . . still watching Little Girl dancing in her heart song . . . and she knew, no matter what Sharon said, she loved us . . . so she asked, "Sharon, can you help me introduce Little Girl to group on Sunday? The only way I can figure this out is to have a heart song to read to the group, but that requires showing you, and I wanted to make sure that was okay . . . If not, I understand.

Also,

Little Girl will be nervous, and will need you or someone else to read as Little Girl and Mom . . . and Barbara will need to hear from you or another voice to feel the heart song deeply and truly.

And Sharon, if we can share on Sunday, Little Girl wants you to pick the heart song. Please don't tell us, because we want to feel the love song most deeply..."

Little Girl is not quite sure about this, but Mom never lies to her. Little Girl could barely stand still . . . so Mom looked at Little Girl and said, "Go ahead . . . you can say it as many times as you want. Sharon loves it when you tell her, Okay?" Little Girl, hardly able to stand still, said, "I love you to the moon and back, Sharon!!!" Then Little Girl started dancing again. Mom just smiled and breathed . . . then she whispered tenderly, "Sharon, I love you most deeply."

BABY STEPS

*L*ittle Girl and Mom read the email from Sharon, and Barbara could tell that Little Girl was so excited and that Mom was a little worried, but Barbara could also tell that Mom could feel Little Girl's joy because she was going to share her heart songs with others soon. Barbara just turned back to her thoughts of Mom, and could tell she was tired, but she would give little Girl another minute to share with Mom. Mom could never take away from Little Girl's heart songs, because Mom knew how happy Little Girl felt about the special gift Sharon had just given her. Little Girl always wanted to talk to Mom about when she shared her first heart song with Sharon, and how Sharon wanted her to share all her heart songs . . . because Sharon told Little Girl that she loved it when Little Girl shared her heart songs with her.

Barbara was always amazed at how tender Mom was with Little Girl. Then the question crossed Barbara's mind, "I wonder why Little Girl wants to share her heart songs so badly?" Then Barbara thought again, "Sharon told us we could take baby steps, or rather, that is what Barbara was willing to do for Little Girl and Mom because Mom wanted Little Girl to dance always.

Barbara could never tell Mom no because she had to admit to herself that she loved watching Mom, and how she could make Little Girl feel.

Baby steps . . . Barbara was questioning the wisdom of letting Mom and Little Girl ask Sharon about their heart songs . . . it was Barbara's job to always protect Little Girl and Mom. Barbara always let Mom come out when someone needed her, especially if it was the Loved Ones . . . and even sometimes for Him. Barbara could always hear Mom talking to Little Girl, and sharing her heart songs about the Loved Ones . . . about the beauty of kindness and tenderness. Mom always seemed so peaceful when she could soothe Little Girl and the Loved Ones. Barbara especially loved to hear Mom talking with the Loved Ones and sharing her heart songs with them because the Loved Ones, at moments, shared their heart songs with Mom.

Barbara then suddenly turned away from the thoughts, because she instinctively knew she must always protect Little Girl and Mom. Barbara had decided that Mom needed to rest, so she picked up her headphones and turned her phone on to listen to music. Barbara knew that Little Girl loved stories, and when Barbara listened to her music, Little Girl would sit for hours to hear the different stories of other's heart songs. When Little Girl listened so intently to hear the heart songs in the music, then Mom could at least rest . . . but not sleep. Mom always wanted Little Girl to hear as many heart songs as possible, because Mom knew how happy Little Girl was when she could other's heart songs . . . and Little Girl could relax, which meant Mom could too.

Barbara walked to the couch and lay down to listen to the music. Barbara knew Little Girl and Mom were safe at the moment, so Barbara allowed herself to ponder her question . . . she just could not figure out why she let Mom ask Sharon about sharing their heart songs . . . It was too soon, and she did not want Little Girl or Mom to get hurt ever again.

Barbara did not realize that Mom was listening intently to her . . . she often did, because Mom wanted to help Barbara feel her and Little Girl's heart songs. Barbara decided after a while to go lay down on the bed, because Little Girl was being very calm. As Mom was drifting into sleep, she thought about Barbara's question, and with the question on her mind she ever so slowly wandered into sleep.

Barbara popped out of bed, looked at her phone and thought, "Damn, only three hours. It's only 5:17am..." She distracted herself with practical thoughts about the day ahead so she would not think about the answer, but Barbara knew that once you know something, you can't unknow it. Barbara knew that is why she protected Mom and Little Girl so much . . . she wanted to stop any ugliness from seeping in to scare them. Mom was so good at painting kindness and tenderness for Little Girl. Barbara also knew that Mom could not paint when Mom was fearful. So Barbara let the answer cross her mind . . . Barbara knew that she wanted to share in Little Girl's and Mom's heart songs. Barbara also knew this meant she could not always protect Mom and Little Girl. Barbara knew that Mom and Little Girl wanted her to share too, but Mom would never make Barbara do anything she was not ready for . . . so Mom just spoke to Barbara and said, "It is time to come share with Little Girl. As long you protect us, we cannot dance with Little Girl in our heart songs . . . and that is what Little Girl wants the most; she wants all of us to dance with her in our heart songs."

Barbara begrudgingly admitted to Mom that she was so tired of protecting all of us from the ugliness and that she knew there was another way, but to take a chance, a leap of faith . . . to be able to dance with Mom and Little Girl . . . So . . . for the first time, in a long time, Barbara let Little Girl's joy come through a little, and that was enough for now. Barbara whispered, "Baby steps, baby steps..." and Barbara, for the first time, added to Little Girl's and Mom's heart songs fully. Ever so softly, Barbara whispered to the universal vibration to connect with Sharon, "I will always love you, to the moon and back and even more deeply."

LEAPT

hen I thought some more about when I said I did not want to share my heart songs with Him...

What I was trying to say is . . .

That I am afraid He will not be tender with the most precious gift I have to give...

And...

I wanted to keep taking baby steps...

And...

53

If I shared my heart song with him, I was afraid it would have been too much to bear if he was less than tender just then . . .

I want to give my heart songs to others without fear, and with Him there always seems to be fear...

And...

That makes me feel sad for him...

But...

Me, I leapt, and I am swaying in my slow dance of joy just now . . .

Because...

I will be dancing freely in my joy with others in the sweetest heart song ever . . . Papa's (Spirit)...

So...

I just smile and breathe and dance slowly and say . . . "I just need a little bit more patience..."

Then I thought of you, and I whispered, "I love you always, to the moon and back, and even more deeply..."

HEART SONGS

*W*e all can sing,
They just can't or won't...

And...

That is everyone's choice,

To sing or not . . .

I choose to sing . . .

Relish in your heart song . . . It is most precious . . . and that is when you shine the brightest for all others to see . . .

And their hearts will be moved and they will also want to sing and dance and share their heart songs . . . with others. Wish I could be there heart to heart, but know I am dancing with you always...

Loving you . . . Me...

THE INTERTWINING

*L*ittle Girl was so excited when she pulled up to Sharon's house she could barely contain herself . . . because at least she knew, and Mom too, that they were going to share a heart song with Sharon, heart to heart, which meant Little Girl could share the dance of their heart song, and feel it most deeply. Little Girl just knew that today Barbara would be able to feel her heart song, even if she could not quite dance yet. Barbara felt Little Girl's joy intertwine with Sharon's heart song, and for a while they got to dance together . . . and Barbara felt Sharon's heart song. Barbara also felt the tenderness of Sharon's heart song . . . this touched Barbara's heart deeply . . . she could not help it . . . and Barbara's heart song became a little stronger. While Sharon shared passages from Mom's favorite story, holding us gently and stroking our hair, wrapping all of us in her heart song . . . Barbara could feel the presence of Papa (Spirit) and how Sharon's tenderness touched Mom and brought Little Girl joy beyond measure . . . And Barbara *leaned in* a little more . . . and just breathed . . . then Barbara wept quietly, tears, silent tears, because she wanted to stay embraced in Sharon's heart song too . . . Then she said silently, hoping Sharon could hear too . . . "Sharon, I will love you always..."

KNOWING

*M*om tried to sleep . . . but couldn't because she was thinking about what Sharon had asked her . . . "If you could do anything in the world today with no thought to money or health . . . what would you want to do?" Mom blurted out something about doing something for others, or even something with her Loved Ones because she thought she had to have an answer *right* then . . . and truly those things did add to her heart songs and did bring her joy. Then suddenly, but quietly, Mom heard a small voice . . . it was HER (all of us together) and she told Mom that what SHE wanted to do more than anything, was to share her heart songs with others . . . and dance with joy always. Mom couldn't quite believe that SHE had even said anything . . . and Mom knew that this might be the true intertwining that she had being searching for . . . for so long . . . it felt like the beginning of a long Good-bye . . . then Mom thought, "No, not Good-bye . . ." It was leaning in softly, trusting, and knowing . . . because in knowing, you truly do know what love is...

THE ANSWER

*A*s I was thinking while lying down, I spoke to myself and decided to find the answer. I am going to try and feel why I expressed my love in those words with you. I thought I knew why . . . but the logical answer that I came to didn't quite ring true to my heart . . . and I knew there was something more to my expression of love to you . . . As I laid there, and drifted inward with that question in my heart, and floated into the innermost part of my Being to see if I could just feel the truth.

"I love you always (Barbara), to the moon and back (Little Girl), and even more deeply (Mom)."

The truth I felt in my heart to be true:

"I love you always (in this moment and beyond), to the moon and back (inward to my Being), and even more deeply (from my Being outward, to share with you and others.)."

Me . . . I simply Love you...

MOMMY

*L*ittle Girl loves to dance, and she was able to do so freely inwardly . . . and sometimes outwardly, but not very often . . . Little Girl could feel that Mommy...was . . . scared . . . and afraid . . . and Little Girl did not know why, but knew that when Mommy got too scared . . . Mommy would run inward and hear all the bad voices in her head. That scared Mommy so, so, much, that Mommy would be unable to stop the attacking and fighting with all the voices screaming in her head and scaring her more.

When Mommy would hear those voices, she would fall into the darkness . . . and sometimes Little Girl would get in the way and that made Little Girl want to run, because the darkness would come crashing through inward, sweeping up Little Girl and carrying her into complete darkness. Little Girl would become so scared because she did not know why Mommy could not feel her heart songs . . . and that scared Little Girl the most...

Little Girl felt frozen in the darkness, because no matter how hard Little Girl tried to share her heart songs the way she shared with Papa (God) . . . she knew deeply and truly that Mommy could never, ever hear her heart songs . . . and Little Girl would feel sad most deeply.

Moments passed and Little Girl was always surrounded by the darkness, except for a small tiny light that was bright enough to keep her attention within that darkness . . . and that made Little Girl not be afraid of the dark as much.

She would talk to the light of her heart songs . . . when she needed it the most . . . when the darkness would come back, in waves, crashing over her . . . Little Girl knew if she just focused on the light and told Papa her heart songs . . . She could bear the darkness . . . just a little bit more . . . And she did...valiantly...

The more Little Girl spoke to Papa of her heart songs, the more courageous she became . . . because although she could not see Papa in the dark, except in that very little light, she could feel his presence . . . and she felt very loved . . . Papa always said not to open her eyes until the darkness passed, and she mostly didn't . . . she would squeeze her eyes so very tightly as she and Papa intertwined to share in her heart song.

When the darkness was the scariest, Papa would ask Little Girl to share one of her heart songs about Mommy. Little Girl loved to share heart songs about Mommy the most . . . because when Mommy couldn't hear her scary voices . . . she could come and play and dance with Little Girl's heart songs, even if Mommy could not feel Little Girl's heart songs fully and deeply.

Little Girl tried so, so, very hard to show Mommy the feelings of her heart songs . . . But Mommy could never quite intertwine with Little Girl . . . Little Girl always told Papa that she could wait . . . because Little Girl knew she could play and dance and try again with Mommy . . .

maybe, someday, Mommy would truly and freely dance with Little Girl's heart songs . . . and intertwine . . . and just BE...

Then . . . it happened in an instant . . . When Little Girl was not looking at the light . . . because she forgot to look, really...

Little Girl felt all alone and she cried as quietly as possible so the darkness could not hear her...

Little Girl began to feel a warm presence surrounding her and she thought it was Papa but she did not look up...

Then, she heard a whisper, ever so softly . . .

"Little one, look at me..."

And Little Girl slowly lifted up her tear stained face and looked straight into her eyes and she said...

"Little one, sweetness," and even more gently, she whispered to Little Girl while looking straight into her eyes so Little Girl could feel her most deeply...

"I will always love you . . . to the moon and back . . . and even more deeply..."

Little Girl knew in an instant that this was the truth, because she knew when she looked into her eyes she saw kindness, and tenderness, and Little Girl felt very deeply that she would never lie . . . she could feel the truth vibrating from her heart and she smiled softly . . . because she knew in that moment who she was...

Little Girl shyly enfolded herself in her arms, heart to heart, and just leaned into her a little bit more . . . because she loved feeling so, so much love . . . She whispered back to her, "Mom, I love you to the moon and back too..."

And Mom held Little Girl just a little bit closer to her heart, so that Little Girl could lean "INTO" just a little bit more . . . and both Mom and Little Girl drifted into just BEing . . . bringing calm and peace to Little Girl . . . to unconditional love...

To My Beloved Mother

Sharon asked me to write a letter to my mom expressing my feelings about her and me...

*T*o my Beloved Mother, who I love so deeply and simply...

I am trying to find the words of love I have for you always in my heart, in my heart songs, that are uniquely ours, to sing together when leaning in together fully, when intertwining softly can truly begin . . . creating new heart songs that are distinctively ours to share in the joy, tenderness and all that love truly is . . . radiating brilliance . . . for all others to share in . . . in the calming of Being . . . interweaving . . . knowing true love is always loving simply, deeply, and . . . always . . . in shared moments and beyond . . . going inwardly, bursting outwardly, to share in the brilliance of all others . . . in the presence of God.

We, meaning you, me, and all others, have our own unique gift for discovering what our purpose in BEing truly is and always will be . . . the path to discovering is in the choices each of us make on our footpaths of seamless moments . . . choosing willingly and freely . . . not getting lost in the details and with the answer always prompting us . . . inviting us into the calmness . . . allowing us to ask with an open heart . . . for the answers to our heart's questions . . . and allows for the choices that resonate the truth from the core of our hearts . . . and will ever so slowly seep in, and in an instant you will know . . . feeling with your heart deeply . . . the answers to the questions that you carry in your heart.

The trials and tribulations we each carry into our own personal darkness, feeling lost, not seen, and all alone in the deepest chasms of our hearts, will lift when searching for the gift of the answer in the mist of unknowing . . . slowly, step by step, out of the darkness . . . feeling, with your heart, the tenderness that has always been in the rifts of the darkness, waiting patiently, lovingly, tenderly, for us to slip out of the cloak of fear we hold so closely to keep the darkness from spreading more deeply into our BEings . . . allowing for the light of truth and simple love to slowly peek through to speak to our hearts, prompting each of us closer to calmness and peace within . . . to shed the darkness and step into the brilliance we and all others are.

My beloved mother, I know that each of us, in our choices, have struggled to find the true answers to the questions of each our hearts . . . of the trials and tribulations we feel we must carry in our hearts . . . because of the unknowing . . . and in the unknowing, there can never be true understanding . . . until we have the courage to see and feel the truth in our hearts . . . just know that each trial and tribulation is a gift to help us find the complete answer each of us seeks . . . and know that each trial and tribulation we feel we must bear is simply a stepping stone to Greatness.

Love always leaves a significant mark. Know that each of us came into BEing to share in simply loving, without limitations. I know in this moment, I can feel your pain deeply, and that you are confused . . . but Trust in God and in all his wisdom, no matter how small or insignificant you believe you are . . . you are most precious to him and all others, and especially to me.

My prayer for you in my heart is that Love can grow gradually to fullness . . . and that you find the richness in the uniqueness of you . . . so that the unique colors of your BEing can shine with brilliance, intertwining with all others . . . dancing in joy and tenderness with other's heart songs . . . that each of us share willingly and freely.

Mom, I have searched deeply to express my truest heart song so that you can clearly understand what my heart speaks to me to be true . . . I do not know how to accurately let the words flow from my heart in this moment, so I will share a passage that profoundly and deeply spoke to my heart and gave me the courage to trust and lean into the presence of God . . . to give truly, lovingly, deeply, willing, and freely of all that simply loving is.

"Mom, if anything matters, then everything matters. Because you are important, everything you do is important. Every time you forgive, the universe changes; every time you reach out and touch a heart or a life, the world changes; with every kindness and service, seen or unseen, my purpose is accomplished, and nothing will ever be the same."

Mom, I love you most simply

FEELING ME

I was trying to explain the feeling of Love when I felt it actively in my body to Sharon . . . I struggled...this is what I came up with...

God loves you...

Sharon loves you...

You are blessed...

You have everything you need...

There is nothing to fear...

You have everything to be grateful for . . .

Simply loving and knowing . . . in the presence of God . . . Calming . . . spreading from center of being . . . slowly radiating outward . . . moving forward, stretching down my limbs . . . tilted face upward, and in the moment a rush from inward, radiating forth to the presence of God . . . feeling intertwining . . . reverently, tenderly, lovingly . . . for a moment . . . Feeling . . . light . . . feeling joy . . . feeling home . . . feeling . . . simply loving . . . Sharing . . . Loving simply with ALL others...in this moment...

There is more . . . I am unable to quit . . . the words flow to feeling . . . outward to share...

Sometimes I will feel differently but the same . . . a sweeping up from the heart through my face . . . skyward toward the universe . . . feeling . . . love is powerfully washing through me . . . especially when I am touching others to share . . . like this morning . . . when my daughter slept next to me . . . brushing against me . . . in the moment . . . and love swept through me most intensely . . . to embrace her in this moment . . . to fill our hearts . . . with joy . . . happiness . . . unconditional love . . . in the moment of sharing . . . especially with her . . . and all others...

She has such a tender spirit...

I will keep trying to find the words to describe . . . feeling in the moment . . . and share . . .

MY CHILDREN

This email is in regard to a conversation I had with Sharon about my children . . . the next day I was going through my deck of Real Love cards and read . . . so I emailed Sharon to clarify my feelings of the expression of love for my children...

*T*he card:

Falling in Love is the relatively equal and abundant exchange of imitation love . . . A formula for disaster...

This made me ponder our conversation when we were talking about my children . . . when I was trying to describe how deeply I loved each of them . . . Then I uttered the words, "I am in love with them." It didn't sit right with me from the moment I said it, because that was not what I was trying say . . . I love each of them for who they are . . . for their uniqueness, kind spirits, their glow and the sharing of their gifts . . . how their presence is a gift to the world . . . and we are all blessed in that sharing . . . they and all are so beautiful...

Welcome to my world . . .

STARRY NIGHTS

Starry Nights is a letter I wrote to my co-workers for all the support given to me throughout my treatment for cancer . . . I never did share with them . . . for some this will be the first time seeing it . . . I was too afraid to share and risk being judged . . . so I shared with Sharon instead...

*H*ave you ever on a starry night looked up into the sky and just looked?

The more you gaze, the more stars you see. The stars begin to transform, and seem to dance in the sky, and certain stars begin to catch your eye.

Then your focus is on those bright dancing stars, and it is hard not to look; they have your attention. As you focus more intently, you discover that among the bright dancing stars there are other stars that shine even brighter.

You become captivated, and thoughts unfold as you watch and absorb the brightest stars.

Each star is beautiful, unique, enchanting, and awe inspiring.

Then you come to the realization that the universe is immense, full of wonderment, and it is humbling to be in the presence of such influence.

Your heart swells with gratitude for the opportunity to have this moment in time to experience and absorb the impact those stars have on you.

THE JOURNEY FROM ROSE COLORED GLASSES

I wrote this in third person to Sharon . . . this piece is about when my husband uttered the words to me, "You wear rose colored glasses." These words . . . took me into a downward spiral . . . and I felt so unseen and not loved . . . I was in so much pain . . . and naturally I blamed him . . . much easier that way...now I know differently...

*I*n the midst of His attack, he uttered words that did not speak to my vessel (body), or to my mind (knowings), but to my heart . . . where our most precious gifts are stowed away to share with others in the loving moments that seem to be so fleeting . . . the gifts of my love and tenderness are given freely.

"You always see the world through rose colored glasses..." That is all I heard . . . I closed my eyes and I went inward . . . Little Girl was scared . . . and Mom was frightened of losing our most precious gifts, and that made Barbara fight back valiantly . . . But we got lost in the details and became selfish with our most precious gifts . . . and forgot to freely share with Him too.

Little Girl stood in the darkness so He could not see her, but Mom was weeping, wishing we would stop . . . but the tears she couldn't hold back seeped through the vessel for Him to see . . . and that, for some reason I could not understand, made him want to fight even more . . . Barbara could feel Mom's sadness and that made her stop and just be quiet in the details going on around them. Barbara knew if she stopped . .

63

. breathed . . . they could center and just BE . . . and that would calm Little Girl so she would come and just BE too. So Barbara closed our eyes and breathed . . . and breathed again . . . and slowly as Barbara kept breathing, gently Little Girl came to intertwine with Mom and Barbara . . . and I wept . . . because of the knowing . . . the knowing that the divide was even greater now.

We, meaning all of me, loves to share our heart songs with others, especially with The Loved Ones (my children), because when I do, I see and treasure the gifts The Loved Ones share with me freely . . . love and tenderness . . . Little Girl calls our gifts "heart songs" . . . and heart songs are our favorite thing to share in the whole universe and beyond, because there is such love and freedom, joy and happiness, and Little Girl always got to dance freely when our heart songs intertwined with The Loved Ones . . . Mom and Barbara loved it when Little Girl could dance, and that made me feel peaceful.

The walls Barbara built were meant to keep the ugliness out and keep us safe. Mom thought of those walls often, and softly, and would talk to Barbara and Little Girl to see if they were ready to share heart songs with others so The Loved Ones could share more deeply in our precious gifts . . . Little Girl knew what was lurking out there, and she was very afraid, but Barbara would always say, "Little Girl is not ready yet . . . she does not want more darkness seeping inward. So Mom just said okay . . . I can be patient.

Mom looked and looked for the one thing that would help Little Girl feel safe enough to share our heart songs, but she could never quite find the answer . . . she found bits and pieces of the answer, but nothing seemed to coax Little Girl from stubbornly holding tight to our heart songs . . . so Mom would put the knowings away for now, to see if they might be part of the complete answer . . . and she kept on searching, lovingly, any way she knew how, through books, school, counseling, seminars . . . Mom would try anything if it meant she could find any partial truth of the gift of finding the answer . . . so Mom was very patient . . . and kept looking.

Many moments passed and we were able to navigate through the details; so well in fact, that we almost forgot about our most precious gifts . . . until one day He asked Barbara to read a book called *Real Love*

64

. . . He said He was worried about her . . . Because He could feel, somehow, that with each piece of the answer SHE found, SHE was drifting farther away . . . We felt it too and we knew we were drifting . . . centering and just BEing . . . and that scared him the most.

Mom, just to make the details stop, said she would read Real Love . . . and she did . . . And saw the truth . . . and the answer was almost complete, but not quite yet . . . And Little Girl was excited...And Barbara began to relax . . . just a little...and Mom wanted to trust completely . . . not just immensely.

He asked Barbara if she would be willing to go see a Real Love coach with Him . . . Barbara said okay . . . We did not know what to expect . . . but Mom was open to whatever the answer might be . . . and we got a warm feeling . . . and Mom knew what that meant . . . that they were on the right path . . . Mom said to us that we just had to be a little bit more patient . . . we could do it...we were willing to do it . . .

Barbara walked into the house . . . the coach seemed nice enough and engaging . . . this made us relax and talk freely, but not to freely because He was there, and we did not want to upset Him and say the wrong thing. Mom wanted to look into her eyes . . . she needed to *see* . . . and Mom looked, and saw something, but she was not quite sure what . . . but Mom had an inkling . . . and she began to trust a little more.

Barbara kept going to the coaching sessions with Him because she wanted to believe so desperately . . . she could feel just within our grasp the key to the answer . . . and Mom was hesitant to trust, but it was growing, growing . . . and then, in an instant, she trusted immensely.

Barbara thought this would be the answer and the work could begin . . . but Barbara decided to go to a session by herself, because He really did not want to go . . . but Barbara really did, because she was searching...

As Barbara walked into the house to have her session, she saw a book laying on the table, and picked it up . . . she read the back cover of the book . . . and we got that *knowing* feeling . . . and the coach chimed in and said it was a really good book and that Barbara should read it. Barbara knew that this book, if we looked beyond the details and just *felt* it, would change everything . . . and Barbara read the book . . . and that created a shifting in us . . . because the passages in the book spoke to our whole Being . . . and thus the true journey began.

The very next day, Barbara decided to go to a Real Love seminar, because Mom wanted to feel the presence of just BEing . . . simply and quietly . . . And the coach's voice, heard spoken out loud, could calm us into just BEing, so we went and sat quietly . . . and listened . . . and it was lovely, but not quite right. As Barbara was walking out, she wanted to talk to Sharon for just a moment . . . but before Barbara could get anything out . . . Sharon looked straight into her eyes and straight into Mom's heart, and said, "You are so tender right now." That is when Mom trusted her completely, and the unraveling and the intertwining began...

Sharon,

I love you ALWAYS, to the moon and back, and most deeply . . .

I love you simply...

MY MOM

This particular email is lengthy, as I address my mom and the sexual abuse in my childhood . . . it is almost two separate emails . . . but not...

Seeing any person suffer, due to their own choices, or by no fault of their own, is difficult. My mom's suffering is made up of a little of both . . . because of the choices she's made that govern her life. She does not want to take responsibility and wants to blame everyone and everybody for everything. My brother has spoken extensively with her about the choices that each person makes, and how each choice has a bearing on the next choice and so on . . . He explained to her that because of the choices she's made, she is where she is . . . and not because people have done this to her. She does not want to hear that . . . and does not want help for her mental illness . . . her choice. I understand this. It is my mom's choice to be where she is in her life. There is nothing I can do to ease her pain for her . . . nor do I want to. It is more of just knowing her life could be so much more, and she cannot see that. I love her, and I hope she can find some solace in her choices.

MOLESTATION . . .

The molestation started when I was about three and went on until I was fifteen, when I told him, "No more." My sister actually punched him when she was around the age of fourteen, and that is when it stopped for her. It happened every time we had to go and see them. My mom would force us to go, even though my sister and I begged and pleaded with her not to make us. I did not realize until much later, that my mom never asked me why I did not want to go . . . she was so wrapped up in her own wants and needs that she could not be bothered to even wonder as to why her daughters did not want to go. I am not talking about just requesting . . . I remember begging her to not make me go . . . she never did ask why.

My sister and I slept in a different room than the boys. He would then send everybody to bed around eight, including his wife. My sister and I slept on a pull-out sofa bed, and we never talked because we knew what was coming and we couldn't say anything . . . we were both terrified. I would sit and listen for him to come down the hall, waiting and waiting . . . and it was pure terror when I could hear him coming. When he entered the room, he would disrobe, and in the side door of the nightstand he would get out the petroleum jelly and choose one of us girls to molest first. If it was my sister, I would just close my eyes and go inward, and sing to myself and try not be present when he was molesting her. He then would come to me (or her), sometimes just being really perverted in the sense of stroking my body . . . and I hated him touching me . . . and I especially hated it when he touched my sister . . . I could sense how afraid and really mad she was all the time. I only remember bits and pieces . . . the cologne he wore, BRUTE . . . and a robe, baby blue. He had no regard for us and he never said anything. It was so quiet, except he always kept the TV on down low. Sometimes he would be done quickly, and sometimes he would take hours . . . that's all I can truly recall.

There is so much more abuse . . . I started to make a list of people from my childhood who abused me either physically, mentally, or sexually . . . and even spiritually . . . The list is long.

I also made a mental list of all the people I can remember who, for whatever reason, were a part of my childhood . . . and taught me lessons about the beauty of every person . . . who performed acts of kindness that showed me I was worth fighting for . . . that loved me for me and did not abuse me. Those acts of love toward me as a child and young adult, have been what has kept me, for the most part, grounded in gratitude, and wanting to do the same for others. If I can only help someone to feel unconditionally loved, then I know my suffering was not in vain but a blessing . . . to be able to understand and to be able to connect with people who need it the most.

RESPONSIBLE

Sometimes I have such moments of clarity . . . This was one of those times...I could sum my feelings up honestly and straightforwardly . . .

I thought about how I am feeling some more...
Simply put . . .

I am tired of feeling that I am responsible for others. I want to be me . . .

Love you, sweet lady . . .

HOW ARE YOU?

This was written after my stay in the hospital in isolation for radiation treatment . . . my memory is foggy here . . . I seem to be all over the place . . . Sharon was checking in on me...

I am having a lot of negative feelings towards both myself and Him. Understanding now how both of us, although well intended, have been selfish and unloving and caused damage. I am actually really feeling a lot of resentment toward Him . . . I am not blaming Him . . . but

68

I am not blind to his inconsideration toward me . . . and I have told myself on many occasions that I chose this, and accepted this behavior from Him because ____ fill in the blank . . . I am afraid of dealing with his temper . . .

I did not want to fight with Him over the kids in a divorce because I truly believed it would be more about Him trying to keep the kids away from me to hurt me, and not what was in the best interest of the kids. I knew that if I had divorced Him when the kids where younger, that I and the kids would have paid for it on many levels . . . from my mom, his mom, his brother, and Him.

I did make choices that I thought were in the best interest of the kids and me . . . to be safe and get where I needed to go to get out . . . I also was hoping somewhere that he and I at some level could maybe make things work . . . it was always short lived though.

How are you feeling being home?

TRAPPED BY CHOICES MADE...

How are you feeling about Him?

One minute I am done, this cannot be, and the next, I am berating myself for being selfish in my attitude toward Him and being unloving.

I talked to my sister last night, and I told her I did not want to stay here with Him . . . and I felt wrong about feeling that way. I told her I did not want a divorce right at this moment (I think) and was thinking about a separation . . . so He and I could give each other space, so we could see more clearly, and not influence each other with our behaviors.

She thought it was a good idea but that my timing was off . . . She suggested I wait until my daughter finished high school or turned eighteen . . . that way He couldn't put her in the middle of whatever we decided to do.

She also thought He would not let our daughter and I stay in the house while she finished high school without Him being there . . . but He could stay at His brother's house, which is basically empty most of the time. My sister said that maybe he would come to this on his own, and then she said, "Have you talked to Sharon?"

"Nope, not yet"

My focus needs to be on healing my body for the next few months . . . The hospital called and said I had to stay on this special diet because I have to do more testing and possibly more treatment . . . the next scan is in three or four weeks . . . then I will have more information on what the rest of my treatment will be. The cancer was more than expected . . . that is why I was given a higher dose.

My brothers are here visiting and I, for the first time, am being very open with them, not worrying what they might or might not think of me or Him. It is nice to share all of me with them . . . and I am learning so much about them and how they view me and our childhood and everything . . .

I guess we have a lot to discuss . . .

AFTER TODAY

*A*fter today...
I do not want to continue this way.

I know in my heart I will never, ever be able to be *ME* with Him . . . no matter how I look at it. I either chose Him and die from the inside out, or choose to live and thrive and walk through the pain . . . either way there is pain . . . I can no longer protect myself or convince myself that I am saving others from pain . . . I have known this for a while, but have never spoken directly to knowing my inner truth . . . I know and feel that this is a choice I must make in order to live my life with passion and purpose . . . I am tired of trying to spare others from being hurt . . . and in reality that is what I have done . . . I thought I was doing the right thing . . . Now I know better . . . I now know that it is selfish to work from fear and being afraid . . . I am trying to listen to my voice instead of ignoring it . . . it was a mistake to do so in the past, and I am not willing to do so anymore . . . I cannot run from what is so blatantly obvious to me . . . I will always love Him, but I will never, ever be able to trust Him completely . . . He does not get me . . . or care too . . . That is no longer acceptable for me . . .

Love you much...

70

INTENTIONS

I am just feeling . . . like I need to journal to you...

So, I am struggling with not just blurting out to Him my intentions . . . I am lying . . . I do not want to wait, but that is what I need to do . . . I need to not act recklessly when I am responsible for the expression of my choices. It feels like I am not living with integrity. Then I think about it some more, and understand that I am not the only one to be effected by my decisions. My brother said it is obvious that we (He and I) have been living parallel lives for quite some time . . . I wish I was braver before . . . But I will not wallow in my past choices . . .

It is what it is, and I will move forward, trying to listen to my inner voice and being who I need to be . . . not worrying about what others think or feel about me . . .

I love being me . . . sharing . . . caring . . . loving . . . seeing beauty, gratitude, blessings . . . it is not wrong to be me . . . this I know to be true. I know I will stumble, crawl, cry, cause pain, feel pain . . . that some will embrace me and some won't . . . I know when I love . . . it is real . . . it is all of me . . . not just parts of me . . . and I can feel the peace and love, and build relationships . . . in complete trust . . . I do not think I could go back. I know I could not go back to convincing myself to live in mediocrity . . . I know to the core of my being . . . I am so much more than settling . . . I am excited . . . for what will unfold . . . As I follow my heart, it gives me the strength and courage, and stretches me to discover parts of me that have lay dormant and ignored for so long. I know I will have whispers that speak to me, and at other times I will be screaming . . . finding me . . . is so beautiful . . . seeing others . . . is such a blessing . . . I am loved, and in that, I can love freely . . . it seems so simple . . . Letting go . . . and opening . . . stretching . . . I am grateful and feel so blessed and am so happy I can share with you . . . I am getting sappy . . .

Love you . . .

"So, What Are You Going to Differently?"

This is my response to a question Sharon asked me.

$\mathcal{L}$ ove freely, live authentically, know that I am worth fighting for . . . my dreams and voice are just as precious as everyone else's and there is room for my truth . . .

Stay inspired . . . random acts of kindness . . . share . . . love more deeply . . . keep seeing the beauty . . . keep being grateful . . . recognize that I am blessed . . . loved . . .

Humbled to be able to have the ability and capacity to even contemplate my feelings . . . the human experience is such a wonder, and full of possibilities . . . I love sharing my experiences . . . and me . . . with you and others, growing and expanding and stretching . . . and FINDING THE COURAGE TO TELL MY TRUTH . . .

I love you . . . ALWAYS.

Do I Still Believe?

$\mathcal{I}$ stop and think . . . Do I still believe in miracles? Miracles are everyday acts of kindness . . . a connection in an instant . . . a smile . . . a knowing . . . someone understanding me in that moment . . . it brings peace . . . an understanding of knowing I am not alone . . . it brings me to my knees . . . tears flowing . . . because in that moment, I do believe . . . I am loved . . . unconditionally . . . I am not alone . . . How can I resist being me? Why is it such a struggle? Why the questions? Listen to my voice I say, don't question . . . leap of faith . . . The thought that I am loved flitters through my mind . . . I ponder . . . What is there to ponder? It is or isn't . . . embrace it . . . waiting for me . . . leaning in . . . accepting . . . there is nothing to prove or fix . . . just Be . . . I am loved . . . and am loving . . . I am worth fighting for . . . I am not wrong to want to share my heart . . . I want to be me . . . it matters to me. I want to touch others and give back as much as I have been given . . . and then some more . . . it is important to me to be able to reach out . . . however that might look . . . I do not know, and it doesn't much matter, as long as I am being me...WHY IS THIS SO HARD? Maybe because I am afraid of being labeled . . . I HATE LABELS...

But I Love you...

PEOPLE

I wrote this to Sharon . . . the essence of what I was sharing with her about a presentation I had to give for part of my final for a class I was taking...

*T*onight I talked about living to our passion, however that is defined . . . being honest and being authentic.

I love sharing with people, encouraging them, supporting them, watching them grow . . . it is amazing to me . . .

I am blown away by what people have experienced and come through, and how they choose to live authentically . . . I know we all make mistakes, and I know we all stumble . . . I know that we all suffer pain, cause pain . . . what is amazing is the grace, courage, humbleness, and love in which people chose to live through life experiences. It gives me hope . . . encourages me to try a little harder, to keep stretching when all I want to do is quit . . . I know in those moments, that this is when I have to try even harder . . . this I know to be true . . . I am not exactly sure where I will end up . . . but I am willing to try and see and experience my choices . . .

THE LIE

This particular piece is hard for me to share because I do not want to paint anyone with a skewed paint brush...I hesitate, and question if this is the truth . . . then my thoughts run to..."It is *MY* TRUTH," because it is my memory of the viewpoint I had at that age.

*S*o, I am going to share a flashback that has been reoccurring for me ever since I made the decision to leave Him . . . (Which I have not told him about yet...) "The lie" . . . it stirs up the feelings of this event in me, and it is hard to process the pain when I'm not living

73

authentically from my heart . . . I have shared in group and discussed it, but it still lingers...

My mom had a method of punishing us when we were smaller that was less than kind . . . I (we/triplets) was eight years old and my little brother was four. At the time of this incident, I had a step-sister, who I believe was seven . . . or maybe nine . . . it does not matter.

My mom never punished us when her husband was home . . . they took turns beating us for whatever infraction when the other wasn't there (that's another story though). This particular time, it was more intense . . . someone had taken a steak knife and stabbed the leather couch . . . and basically destroyed it . . . We all know who did it . . . my step-sister . . . that girl had rage in her like you would not believe. My mom was so mad that the couch was ruined, and she wanted my step-sister to admit she had done it. My mom wanted to break her. My step-sister was stubborn . . . very, very stubborn.

We were all lined up . . . shoulder to shoulder . . . my mom would hit us every two to three minutes. For each spanking that one of us received, the person who finally confessed would have to take that number of whippings as a punishment for making the others suffer the beating . . . My step-sister would not confess . . . she was stubborn, but I could also tell she was very afraid of my mom . . . we had gone through maybe five or six rounds of being hit, when I looked at my four year old brother and saw that he would not be able to handle much more, and my heart broke. I stepped forward and said that I had done it. My mom grabbed me and dragged me down the hall to her room, where she made me strip down and proceeded to beat me with some object as she made me count how many times I was being struck. I did not scream, but I did cry silently, which pissed her off . . . so I got through that, and thought I was done . . . but she yanked me by my hair and told me that because she knew I was lying, she was going to teach me to never to lie to her again . . . She then doubled the beatings from thirty to sixty . . . I went inside . . . I do not know what happened after that...

I knew in that moment that my mom did not love me, and wanted to control me . . . and that I had to survive, because I was not going to let this woman destroy me . . . so I endured what I had to to survive . . . to thrive . . . I felt alone . . . and I wanted someone to love me for me . . . to

74

see me for me . . . I walk in that fear when I interact with Him and his anger . . . I want to run . . . he does not see me . . . I am scared . . . I will endure what I must to thrive...

I BELIEVED...

I wrote this to share in group. I wanted to share that there are people who have touched my life in positive ways . . . and left a significant mark on me . . . feeling loved and accepted . . . these people when remembered warm my heart . . . and I can feel love even today...

I am grateful for the people who have touched my life and made me believe...

The first person I remember who cared about me was Mr. Pageant, my 4th grade teacher. He hugged me when I was teased, and played with me when I was lonely. He told me I was special and I believed...

Mrs. Montgomery, my 5th grade teacher said I was smart . . . and I believed her . . .

The lady next door when I was about eleven, pulled me aside and had me look in the mirror, and told me I was beautiful from the inside out . . . I believed...

Bishop Moss told me when I was thirteen that I was precious, and a strong, beautiful young lady. He helped me through some very hard times . . . he believed, which made me believe . . .

My high school teacher in psychology, whose name escapes me but who I can see in my mind's eye, said I had an "old soul" and that I was loving in a way that most souls never could be . . . he taught me to listen to my heart, and believe in kindness and love...

I let that young girl go who believed in me so much . . . love, kindness, tenderness, compassion . . . because that is what I believed I had to do . . . I always thought and thought of love, kindness, tenderness, and compassion, and every once in a while I would step forward to act . . . but then retreat when I was told not to be that way . . . I was told I needed to focus on the reality of life...I am not blind to the ugliness . . . because I got to experience so much on such a personal level from a young age . . . I just wanted to focus on the light in the world . . . it gave me the courage to take the next step and believe...in love, kindness, tenderness, and compassion . . .

Then I met you . . . you told me I could be me . . . and not to hide but share, walk in the pain, because there is healing . . . holding my hand and showing me it is okay to be me . . . And I started to believe again...

I will ALWAYS have a special place in my heart for those who believed in me because without them, I would not have the courage to be me . . . I love you.

I'VE LEARNED

I wrote this to Sharon after contemplating everything I had experienced through Real Love Community . . . up to this point . . . coming to an awakening of who each us are...

I've learned that there is no perfect time for LEAPS of FAITH . . . just leap and grow . . .

I've learned that LEANING IN is the best gift I can give myself . . . I believe again . . .

I've learned that the TRUTH can set me free . . .

I've learned that my THOUGHTS are my REALITY . . .

I try to look for beauty in all that I see...

I've learned that in LETTING GO . . . I can expand and grow...

I've learned that the only person I can make HAPPY is myself . . . I will strive to always choose happy . . .

I've learned that whoever gives and receives KINDNESS in any form, is good for the soul . . .

I've learned that MISTAKES are stepping stones to greatness . . . don't fear mistakes . . . grow with mistakes.

I've learned that REACHING OUT and touching someone is a precious gift to share . . . people love everyday acts of kindness. Smiles, hugs, kind words, a simple courtesy...

I've learned I will ALWAYS have something to learn...

I've learned that ORDINARY people can do extraordinary things...

I've learned that I am responsible for my destiny . . . I can make all my choices (YEAH!!!)...

I've learned that tenderness, LOVE, and compassion were meant to be shared . . . I love sharing...

I've learned that people may not always remember my words or acts, but they will always remember how I made them feel . . . I will make every effort to choose KINDNESS in actions and words...

I've learned that everyone is a unique, DIVINE Being, who gets to choose how to live each day . . . I choose to write my story with love...

I've learned that GRATITUDE stretches my heart . . . growing and expanding to include others . . . finding joy and happiness and all the kindness I have received...

I've learned that LOVE IS EVERYTHING . . . And that is where I want to be . . .

THEN WHAT?

Okay . . . this memory is coming up a lot lately...

I was in junior high, and I had to ride the bus . . . this particular morning there were no seats except towards the back, where the kids that caused trouble sat. I tried to ignore their comments but it was almost impossible and the words I do not remember...

The thing that was unkind was that the boy who was sitting behind me thought it would be funny if he could set my pants on fire. I did not know what was going on because I was trying to ignore them . . . my mistake.

I had some cheap cotton pants on and the lighter he was using singed and burned holes in the back of my pants from the top of my waist to the top of my bottom . . . I was lucky . . . by the grace of God I did not get burned . . . not even a little...

They were all laughing at me . . .

I did not react . . . I just sat there . . . I could not believe this was happening to me . . .

The bus got to the school, and I walked to my choir teacher's room . . . I just looked at her and she looked at me and I burst into tears . . . it was so unkind and I did not deserve to be treated that way . . . I had done nothing wrong...

My teacher became very angry . . . not at me, at first . . . at the boys . . . then at me, because I would not tell her who did it . . . I was too afraid of being hurt again . . . and I begged her not to call my mom . . . I finally convinced her I was fine and I just wrapped my sweater around my waist...

My mom moved us around so much . . . I went to four high schools . . . three junior high schools . . . and more than ten elementary schools . . .

I would connect . . . find kindness . . . and then be yanked from it . . . it always seemed just out of reach for me . . . If you and I are going to be truthful, I am afraid you and Real Love will be yanked from me . . . then what? It scares me . . .

I MATTER . . . RIGHT?

This is a two part email to Sharon about my experience with a particular group I attended for Real Love . . . although I am not sharing Sharon's responses to me . . . you can see the questions with my answer back, after my sharing with her...

So, I went to group tonight . . . and someone shared about her mom . . . I could barely sit there because I understood what she was saying about her mom. In fact, her share reminded me of similar incidences in my own childhood with my mom, and feeling like I was such an inconvenience in her life. And the older I got, the more attacking my mom was. She really did not like her boyfriends or husbands being nice to me . . . if they were, I was called a whore, a prick tease, a slut . . . you get the picture...

I think what is triggering me is realizing how desperately I wanted my mom or dad to love me, and it just didn't happen. These memories that I try not to think about just reinforce that I had a pretty shitty childhood and I was desperate for attention and love . . . I do not mean that from a victim standpoint, just as a fact. I, at a fairly young age, was able to reason that my mom and dad were not loved by their parents, so that was why they thought it was okay to be that way with me; it was me coping with feeling unloved, and finding excuses to allow myself to keep hoping and loving in my own way, and protecting my brother and sister. I would endure much for them so they would not have too (my perception) . . . I do not understand what drove me to do this; it was just who I was. I try not to think about it too much . . . it is what it is...

Part of my survival mechanism, for whatever reason, was to find the good in everything. I did not turn to anger very often, unless I was pushed to a corner and had to fight; it is not my nature to fight; I always had mom inside of me, especially when I was younger . . . This thinking helped me to cope, to hope, to have the courage to endure the reality of my life.

The thing is, I still look for the light in people and the world. I understand that we have different capacities to give and receive, and we ebb and flow throughout our days . . . lives. I also understand now that this coping skill has become a detriment it comes to making healthy decisions for myself. I want desperately to believe that I am loved, and was willing to make excuses for the unkindness and disregard for my own self, for those fleeting moments of what I thought was acceptance. As I am shifting, I can see this behavior and recognize it more often . . . I am not an object to be thrown away or disregarded. I deserve to be loved . . . and to live as my authentic self...to be true to my voice...

Someone in group asked me a few weeks ago while I was sharing, if I was trying to be perfect . . . I just replied, "No . . . Just me . . . " For whatever reason, this made me want to run . . . but I didn't . . . what happened instead is that I became afraid to share me . . . as this question kept popping up randomly throughout my days which is why I am telling you this . . . . I do not think it is wrong to want to see the light in the world and practice kindness and love. I started feeling as though being me was not right . . . I do not know why this is bothering me, other than maybe it stems from trying to do what other people think I should do so they can be happy . . . I do not know why this person asked me that, and I did not want to have a conversation with that person . . . so I just stopped (running) . . . I am questioning myself a lot, and that is why I have been going to group so much, calling and journaling; I want to share my heart with others . . . But I don't know if it is the right thing to do . . .

I matter . . . right?

My heart matters to me . . . I am still more tender than I thought . . . I want to share . . .

I want to be me . . .

The person I am today is based on my experiences. My experiences are what happen to me . . . every experience gave me a choice to either build myself up or tear myself down. If I got down I would pick myself up, because there was no happiness in being sad or feeling sorry for myself. Life is beautiful and that is what I try to focus on . . . the beauty . . . I ignored the ugliness and made excuses . . . it is time to stop and face reality . . . that I do not have to live with ugliness . . . and I can speak my truth . . . I know my heart best…

My clinginess to people does not serve or contribute to my happiness . . . what I thought was loving and kind . . . taking care of others . . . I now understand is just a form of control . . . manipulation . . . to get the desired outcome to avoid conflict and avoid pain . . . and when I stop and think about it . . . responsibility.

OUR MARRIAGE

This is an entry that I shared with Sharon . . . this is a letter I wrote to my husband. I was struggling to speak my truth . . . I wanted him to understand . . . I was in fear and feeling the need to explain . . .

*W*hat I am about to share with you will not come as a surprise to you. I want to express that I have thought carefully about what I am about to share with you. As we discussed several days ago, being in a relationship will occasionally cause pain, both in the giving and receiving . . . it is the natural consequence of being intertwined with another human . . . nobody is always good or always bad . . . the ultimate choice as to how we react to each other falls to each individual, and not

80

the other person . . . I need to share this information regardless of your choice in behavior . . . it is your choice (reaction), not mine, to make.

Several months ago we had a talk where the seed was planted that the best outcome for us would be to dissolve our marriage amicably. I have thought often of this conversation, and I found a letter from 2007 where you shared with me how unhappy you were and how you felt trapped, and I realized that this cycle has been in our marriage from the get go.

Instead of letting go then, I clung to you even more, and that was absolutely the wrong thing to do . . . I have lied too often, not being honest, by continually being "careful" about what I said in order to protect myself from my fear of being rejected. I also realize that I lie when I do not look at the reality of a situation and rationalize; only seeing the "good" or "bad" in any given situation . . . I have made a conscious effort to try to break myself of this habit. I know that I am attacking in my actions by showing irritation and being distant. My behaviors also have included acting like a victim, acting like I have no choices when I do, and begrudgingly going along when I really don't want to . . . it's wrong to be this way . . . I now know that. I also know that through my behaviors (drowning) I have unintentionally made you feel and hear that I do not love you, and that is unacceptable . . . I now see that too...

I know that we are both drowning in behaviors and are continually blocking each other from living as our true authentic selves...

We have the opportunity and responsibility to ourselves, and to those people who are a part of us, to make the loving choice for ourselves to live from our hearts...and grow and find happiness and inner joy and love, and share with others the happiness from within when living authentically . . . it is a gift to ourselves that will have ripple effects for the betterment of each of our worlds...

I am trying to make the best choices for me . . . I have to believe in myself before I can even think about believing in others. I am choosing to push forward with hope and love, and I have to be accepting of my choices . . . in the end, it is our work to find our self and live and love from our inner joy...

I have made my decision that the most loving act for myself and you is to agree to our earlier conversation to dissolve our marriage amicably . . . I want to do this as peacefully and as lovingly as possible. The choices made on how to proceed will determine if this can be possible.

STAGNANT

I just read about the two seas in the Holy Land. The Sea of Galilee takes fresh water from a nearby brook, and that helps the environment grow and flourish . . . and then the water passes on to the Jordan River, which feeds water throughout the desert, nourishing the land. The second sea, The Dead Sea, takes water from the Jordan River and does not have an outflow . . . it is stagnant.

This example is a perfect analogy for the differences in people. People who live without giving themselves away become stagnant. What they keep stifles them. Those who give freely give of themselves and multiply life.

You reap what you sow.

By enriching others, my life becomes richer. There is joy in giving.

Jon Wesley said, "Do all the good you can, in all the ways you can, to all the souls you can, in every place you can, at all the times you can, with all the zeal you can, as long as you can."

My Life purpose, I think, is to strive to add value for others, to give unselfishly, and to never, ever become STAGNANT.

Love you simply ♥

REALITY

We do not exist in an outer world . . . our reality is our inner world . . . of our creation . . . of our choices (beliefs) made...

Looking at myself . . . changing perception...Regaining my authentic self...

We are all connected . . . (Oneness)...

Journey from mindlessness to becoming mindful in order to uncover awareness . . . finding the TRUTH of who I am...

There is nothing to FIX or feel GUILTY about . . . just being grateful for the gift of learning through experiencing . . .

Faith is everything...

I am responsible for my own HAPPINESS . . . that's it . . . What is really real is LOVE...

TAKES MY BREATH AWAY . . .

*T*he beauty in all of us . . . that surrounds us . . . The sheer power of LOVE and how it has always been present...

Then realizing LOVE is opening your heart to SEE and accept and share . . .

That each person has a journey, and we are here to heal, and help others to heal, in whatever capacity each of us can . . .

That no matter how much darkness we think there is, we all have our inner glow . . . a light to add to the world . . . We are all connected (oneness)...

That Heaven is seeing (feeling) the beauty and Hell is living in FEAR and missing the beauty that Heaven has to offer to us every day . . .

That growth is a conscious choice . . . to have Faith and Believe and yield to our inner voice (Heart) and be committed to a change toward LOVE . . . the power to create loving everyday miracles with all those we come in contact with . . . so many opportunities...

I have ALWAYS been loved and am loved and am Love . . . to choose to share or not, to consciously practice or not . . . it is a choice . . . Very humbling...

BEHAVIORS

So, I am almost laughing out loud as I come to this entry I wrote . . . I remember being upset . . . because I did not want to focus on my behaviors. I just wanted to focus on my feelings . . . I know I was running from them to avoid looking at them . . . Sharon pointed that out to me in an email . . . and this is what I wrote back . . .

L **ying** - earlier this week I started to believe that I was wrong, and that what I was feeling was not real, and those feelings where reinforced by people. I started to believe that my feelings were wrong and I should not share them . . . then I read something that said not to question my feelings and that my feelings were my inner voice (Holy Spirit) trying to communicate with me, and not to convince myself that what I am feeling is wrong . . . don't question, just relax, and feel and act with love...

Saying "No" has been easier than I thought, but the first thing I do is judge myself and say something like, "That was Bitchy," when in reality, I understand it was just speaking my truth. I also question whether the person will like me . . . then I work on telling myself it is their choice to make . . .

Praise - I feel validated and accepted when praised. I start with good intentions, and get praised for something . . . I wasn't looking for praise, but got anyways . . . the issue is, I then tell people, and then it's bragging . . . I understand this about me, and am working on doing acts of kindness anonymously . . . to work through this . . .

Clingy - I was feeling clingy with my daughter because before the Bridal shower, He told me that he went to our daughter's work and told her about the divorce . . . He stated that she was upset . . . so when I went to the shower, I left a little early to speak with her. I asked her if she was upset . . . she said no, and like me, she does not hide the truth well . . . I tried to talk to her, and then backed off because I realized it was the wrong place and time to talk about her feelings about everything . . . my mistake . . . I was just thinking about myself when I came to talk to her . . . I texted her the next day and asked her to lunch or dinner . . . to talk if she wants to . . . Will hopefully happen next week....

84

Running - He spoke to me on Saturday before potluck . . . he thinks I should move out. He said I was different and he could tell the difference in me . . . that I am no longer focused on home but Real Love. He stated that he thought the divorce was the best choice, as we both have been lying and clingy to each other through our whole relationship. I have to agree. He said that my view of the world is off...and that seeing the good in everything is not living in the real world...not his exact words, but the same meaning. I just think that He and I have different perceptions of people and the world.

I avoid Him because I can see that he is sad, and that makes me want to go to him...but I know that is not appropriate right now. I hope he reaches out...he did go to group last Thursday.

I also spend a lot of time listening to music...soothing music...I listen and it brings my feelings up to the surface...sometimes it's peaceful, and other times it brings me to tears . . . sometimes it creates an understanding, and helps me to relate to others, and helps me in the capacity to accept others, and that we all have pain we are living with . . . no one is immune . . . it is part of being human . . . music helps me find my feelings and helps me to connect . . . it may be running . . . for a while...to help me get in touch with my feelings . . . to have the courage to share myself...

Growth is sometimes very painful, but it is a necessary part of moving forward . . . how can I not try to grow? It is always a humbling experience when a person opens his or her heart to being vulnerable . . . to letting the childlike quality of innocence be seen and shared with an open heart . . .

TRUTHS

*R*elax . . . breathe . . . let it be . . . let it go . . . The universe is in perfect order and there is nothing to fear . . . I am loved, I am blessed, and I have everything to be grateful for.

I say this to myself quite often every day. It keeps me closer to peace and helps me to remain calm when life is throwing things around. I focus on trying to show up loving . . . some days that is not so easy.

I had a conversation with Him last night. He came to check on me. I was crying . . . I can't even explain why exactly . . . not because I was sad or angry . . . I don't feel sad or angry at all. I was just lying there on my bed in silence and the tears came . . . I just felt calm . . . but crying . . . so I figured that sometimes I just need to cry even if I cannot identify an exact reason . . . maybe it is for multiple reasons...

I felt like it was a letting go and shifting to a new space . . . truly letting go . . . and I felt humbled and grateful for my life . . . my experiences . . . my childhood, my marriage, kids, and cancer . . . I am who I am because of my experiences, and I cannot express accurately how touched I am to walk through what I have walked through and to be able to finally see the light within myself . . . and seeing and recognizing the childlike innocence in others, and seeing the light in them too. I have come to the decision there is absolutely nothing wrong with me and my view of people and the world. I believe and want to see beauty, which is love, which is God, which is us, which is me in my world. I am the only person who can decide how I want to perceive the world . . . and I choose to do so with love.

With that being said, I am also not ignoring my life and living in la-la land. I interact with people and get triggered into behaviors, feeling like a victim, which our behaviors can stem from. This means to me if we are acting out of anger, clinginess, or lying, running, seeking power, praise, pleasure or safety, we, meaning me, have something to look at within to see what brings this behavior out. It is not avoiding behaviors, but seeing the gift of behaviors as offering me a chance to learn and grow.

I did question for a short while this week, "Why am I letting myself feel so much?" I like feeling, though . . . even if I don't quite have the skills quite yet to gauge where to stop feelings, so they're not always such deep feelings. That is when I start telling myself, "Relax . . . breathe . . . let it be . . . let it go . . . The universe is in perfect order and there is nothing to fear . . . I am loved, I am blessed, and I have everything to be grateful for."

He, for the past week or so, has been kinder to me, and has not attempted to engage me or accuse me of much of anything. He has shifted. He is calm, at least from what I can perceive, and seems accepting of my decision. We talked about, on Sunday, our relationship, and how sometimes relationships were not meant to last forever in the physical sense. I truly believe that He loves me, and I him . . . we just don't have anymore, at least for now, to share, grow, or learn from being together . . . we just are . . . no growth . . . we both need to grow, learn, love to our full capacity and share where we are needed. I told him about all the stuff going on with me, and trying to balance life, and saying no, and taking care of myself . . .

I don't know where I am going, but it feels right to me . . . most importantly, every day in the morning and evening I try to tap into *love* . . . through reading, music, being silent, feeling . . . sometimes for just 15 minutes, sometimes for a couple of hours . . . this is where I can feel me, and feel whatever I am feeling . . . it usually brings me to center, love, gratitude, happiness . . . you know what I mean . . .

I have been contemplating your parenting class . . . something in me tells me that I need to do this . . . I will also be honest and say I am hesitant, because I will have to see myself as the mom I really am, and share the experiences that when I think back on now, make me cringe . . . I will and want to do this . . . it will be quite the journey . . . my children are in my heart, and to expose one's heart is very vulnerable indeed . . . if there are still spots open that is . . .

P.S. I will be more specific with behaviors. I just started typing . . . need to focus . . .

CANCER

*C*ancer, if nothing else, teaches me that I do not have to sweat the small stuff. Dealing with symptoms is just the inconvenience of dealing with the details of healing my body. I am grateful for the opportunity to even have the chance to heal.

I will never ever give up . . . even when I get scared . . . because I do . . . but then I remember who I am . . . and there is comfort in *knowing* that love is all that matters . . . it is constant.

That alone brings me to sane when I go to fear and sit a while . . . . like today . . . I did see and recognized fear . . . it was plain and simple to see that I was afraid of what my body was experiencing and not being able to identify it . . . it brought fear to my thoughts . . . fear of not being able to move forward in my life . . . I forgot that I am loved . . .

I start feeling like I am a burden . . . and not lovable . . . and I do not want to inconvenience people. Being in this mindset even for a short while makes everything seem so much more . . .

Crying because I had fear about speaking up to the doctor who wanted to give me a Vicodin and send me home. I spoke up though, and got the tests to check my white blood cell count and to check the function of my vital organs. I would not have done that a year ago . . .

Because I spoke up, the nurse wanted to research my meds . . . That led him to listening to my symptoms: weakness, insomnia, nausea, cramps, headaches . . . etc. . . . which he found out were all side effects of my medication . . . just knowing that helped me to understand what I was dealing with . . . and gave me courage . . . and strength.. I did not feel strong today . . .

Then I remembered to ask the Universe, kinda praying . . . just asking out loud . . . to have the fearful thoughts that I surrounded myself with today removed . . . and I found comfort in knowing that I am loved by God/Divine (Title) and that I am loved by many and that I love many and that I am safe . . . because I know to the core of my being that what we are is love . . .

HOLLY

Holly is her name, my coach through Cancer Treatment Centers of America . . . and our conversations seemed to always focus on the spiritual side of things . . . This particular day we discussed a book that had shaken me to the core, profoundly shifting me . . . *The Shack* . . . I learned that love leaves a significant mark and nothing will ever be the same again...

$\mathcal{I}$ basically told her that with any encounter we have with others, the core is finding acceptance and love . . . no matter how brief the relationship. That each person comes into our lives for a purpose . . . to give or receive love . . . and to learn and grow from each experience (encounter) . . . that when we all die, we are not counting our material gains but rather focusing on love or the lack of love we each have in that moment . . . and also looking back to recognize loving in our past if not present . . . She said, "That is deep," a lot . . . we talked about the emotional and physical bodies being connected . . . that awareness (mind and heart) of our spirit allows each person to choose unconditional love or not, and to be responsible for our choices. We talked about choosing calm, peace, and happiness . . . It is a choice . . . and so is loving...

We talked about the fact that love is constant . . . when you speak openly and out loud about love, this really makes sense (it really just resonated with me) . . . Love is constant . . . it is in our inner Beingness . . . connecting us with others and God/Universe . . . and it can be seen in some . . . they just radiate, shine, or . . . sparkle...

I told her about Real Love again . . . she asked me if you were trained in Gestalt Therapy. I said I did not know what that was, and she said it sounded like the same principle as Real Love . . . I told her about the books and Greg Baer...

Then I told her that really, there are varying ways in which God/Universe communicates with each person . . . the message is the same . . . love . . . some people just need to hear it in a different format . . . kinda like a coloring book . . . the picture is the same . . . each person can choose how to color it . . . that is love . . . we all have the capacity to have and share it . . . it's just the manner in which we choose to show the colors (talent) ...

I am going on...

Love, Love ♥

FOCUS

While driving to group, I was thinking and feeling about people . . . this is where my thoughts went . . .

*H*ow unique we each are, and how we are each irreplaceable . . . and each person has a purpose that is defined in love. It really does not matter if that person is aware of his or her purpose yet . . . deep down, love is there. That thought alone is so humbling. We each have a talent, a gift to share . . . the potential is staggering to think about. That is what makes each of us so precious...

What we focus on is our reality . . . focusing on goodness . . . leads to being goodness . . . focusing on beauty . . . you find beauty . . . focusing on love . . . you become love . . . There is power in what we focus on . . . Me . . . focusing on kindness, compassion, tenderness, love, and beauty . . . when I'm not distracted by my behaviors. The cool thing I have come to realize is, that even in behaviors, our words will still have the undertone of what we focus on . . . at least for me. I only came to this thought because of something someone said to me today at work.

Behaviors: still feeling clingy but I am okay with that . . . I hold myself back because of feeling like I am being clingy . . . then I think, "That is me now," and that is fine...

Still feeling fear around my health a little, but way, way less . . . I am guessing as I feel better that this will fade away . . . at least I am not dwelling on my health, and hopefully will have some answers tomorrow when I see the specialist . . . we will see. I have a sense of happiness . . . underlying the intermittent thoughts of my health . . .

I feel love and acceptance which makes this whole journey easier to walk through . . . moving forward...

I know I am in choice . . . and that is a freeing thought as well . . . am working on being a different kind of person . . . showing up lovingly...

I LOVE PEOPLE

I truly LOVE people . . . being with them, watching them, engaging with them . . . loving them . . . Beautiful.

I am humbled at all the love that surrounds me, that's offered to me . . . given to me . . . it inspires me, and gives me the courage to move forward . . . to seek unconditional love . . . to give and receive . . . to Be . . . it is so lovely . . . there is a so much beauty in the world . . . I am speechless and amazed how abundant love really is when we stop and see and feel . . . the Universe/God is waiting to explode when hearts open up to unconditional love . . . waiting patiently . . . lovingly . . . to embrace us all . . . love is here . . . within each of us . . . beyond the details, to the core of each of us . . . it is the essence of each BEING . . . we are not alone . . . each of us is connected to wholeness/oneness . . . in unity to share in our love. That each vibration creates an effect in the Universe . . . to be aware of this . . . shows that each of us has the power within us to make an immense contribution to the energy (Love) of the universe. We all have the choice to choose between negative or positive energy . . . creating ripple effects that are endless, that shift the Universe to healing or wounding . . . that one choice alone will decide the movement within our own lives . . . the Universe/God is within all of us . . . to embrace or block unconditional love . . . how the world will look in each moment . . . the choice is just a shift in perception . . . how each person is willing to show up. Love is all that really matters . . . and one can embrace LOVE and strive to live IN love . . . you are then a positive ripple effect . . . lovely...

LOVE, LOVE ♥

CONNECTION AND UNDERSTANDING

I wrote this after spending an evening with my son talking about spiritual awareness . . . it was a very profound, connecting, eye-opening experience as a mom . . . I just walked away with the thought, "Wow . . . he gets it." And my heart swelled with love . . . and I knew no matter what, he would always be fine . . . because he understands our purpose...

*S*o, my son and I were talking the other night about the universal soul. My thoughts keep going back to our conversation . . . that we all have the ability to connect on a spiritual level (non-physical). That is the highest level . . . most people only connect on the physical level. The spiritual level is where we find true happiness because of the connection and understanding of joy and love . . . that it is infinite and unconditional . . . there for each of us to be part of, always. People can ebb and flow from this state. This is the importance of finding one's own way to connect. If one is mindful and practices, it is easier to recognize this state, and then one can consciously choose when to connect and when to untwine . . . to live our lives . . . to experience and learn and grow and share . . . still connected though . . . dimming down . . . that is what I call

91

it . . . to be present and in the moment . . . The knowing that the connections are our individual choices brings inner strength and love to those who are conscious of that choice . . . being part of the universal soul/oneness . . . we all contribute whether knowingly, with intention, or unintentionally . . . no one can escape from adding to the universal soul . . . to not love another is to not love a part of you . . . that is why being mindful (loving) of self-matters . . . continually trying to learn, grow, teach compassion, tenderness, kindness, unconditional love, is a universal truth to me . . . it is at least my purpose...We all have a choice as to how to create ripple effects throughout the universe . . . that impacts us all . . . These thoughts keep coming up in me . . . Maybe a form of running . . . though a beautiful place to have one's thoughts go too . . . that brings a sense of humbleness, reverence, and the understanding of the impact we each have and how we all are continually influencing the universe . . .

Behaviors . . . for me this week I have been in a very mellow state . . . maybe because I'm still feeling I have less than enough energy . . . or maybe I have been focusing on meditating and feeling my feelings . . . this mellowness is just kinda cool to be . . . since I tend to get so busy . . . so I am enjoying . . . and just being and experiencing . . .

Love, Love ♥

BE WILLING TO SHIFT

*B*eing willing to shift (focus/perception) allows us to touch hearts . . . don't try and figure out or control . . . let the moments flow . . . be guided or prompted by your heart or holy spirit . . . as you listen, healing will begin with you and spread outward as the vibrations move into space and time to touch others . . . as we all are connected . . . and as each person heals, so does the Universe . . . creating ripple effects from one another, washing over each of us . . . creating love . . . compassion . . . tenderness . . . kindness...

Softening hearts with each connection/vibration . . . the power of love that each individual can contribute to the universe is our own responsibility to see . . . look . . . feel . . . act . . . love . . . to nurture oneself, to practice unconditional love, will add to the expansion of love .

. . loving, than, is a conscious choice . . . that we make moment to moment...

I wrote this prayer . . . to help me . . . I read it every time I am consciously connecting with people . . . in other words . . . before work, before group, before sharing one-on-one, before calls . . . you know, all the time...

Please help me to be accepting of people...

To love them unconditionally no matter how they show up in my life . . .

To remember each person is the gift of a relationship to learn from . . .

Help me find the words to express my heart authentically and with love . . .

Please help me find or see opportunities to give and receive love...

To help heal and build an understanding of your purpose . . . Unconditional love . . .

Please give me the strength and courage needed to step forward when called...

And to continually move forward in growth . . . to opportunities to remember . . .

Relax . . . Breathe . . . let it be . . . let it go . . . to practice unconditional love...

To remember that the universe is in perfect order and there is nothing to fear . . .

To remember I am loved, I am blessed, and have everything to be grateful for . . .

THE CHOICE

To work through this I have to share my thoughts . . . to release and move forward . . . of interactions I have had over the past several days . . . I have been calling people . . . unable to make clear what I am trying to say . . . need to write it out . . . I wish I knew how to talk eloquently about the

importance of loving our inner child . . . unconditional love starts within us, loving ourselves. Details (spoken words) get tangled and the message is lost in translation. Writing thoughts brings clarity and sharing simple . . .

*T*elling the truth creates opportunities for others to *see* us, which creates the opportunity to make the choice of acceptance . . . and in acceptance there is love. Telling the truth teaches us to stretch our faith in love (others), and as we practice telling our truth, the cloak of fear will feel lighter and will eventually be shed . . . allowing us to walk . . . no to *run*, towards joy, happiness, and love. It takes courage and faith to leap forward without fear and to be willing to make mistakes. In the mistakes there are lessons to learn. We find that leaping into faith will open our hearts and eyes to more choices, and when there is no fear, there is no blaming. This choice to leap into Truth will bring us some measure of happiness and connection (love) with others.

The other part of leaping into faith and telling the truth, is taking responsibility of those truths. We need to not only share our truth, but also take action with the truth. This means self-loving . . . it starts there. We cannot truly feel the full capacity of love if we ourselves cannot love our inner child. We need to continually strive to have understanding of unconditional love toward self, and ask for what we need . . . and not limit ourselves to feeding our fears of helplessness and hopelessness to the child who can hear and feel every thought we have. Surround yourself with fear and you will then see fear in the world. Surround yourself with beauty (love) and you will see beauty in everything . . . it takes courage and faith to shift from fear to beauty (known to unknown). By choosing to shift, you decide where you live continually . . . heaven or hell . . . from one perception to another in an instant . . . it is a practice of conscious choice . . . when we see choices . . . we then have responsibility . . . look, see, feel, act (love).

We have the choice to move toward unconditional Love . . . which includes self-love . . . creating ripples of tenderness, kindness, compassion, and love for self and others...

OR

We can walk in fear, feeling unworthy, alone, afraid, and feeling unloved . . . It all starts with the choice to take responsibility for our truths.

IN THESE EMOTIONS

*T*his past week I have gone through these emotions . . . impatience with Him. He is finally leaving this Sunday . . .

I find myself irritated with his quips and remarks . . . which means I am not feeling loved enough in that moment . . . so I shut the door and feel better . . . I am relaxing . . . I feel content and mellow and in the moment . . . just being . . . very calm . . . At work I tend to think about life . . . how grateful I am . . . how I am making and acting on the best choices for me . . . which builds my optimism and feeds my happiness . . . which fills me with eagerness to pursue my passion and share my heart . . . when I share my heart, I experience joy and love. In these emotions I am also walking through feeling like a victim, but not wanting to . . . I go from a level of anger that is so distracting that I do not stay there, to a low level of running away by shutting the world out for a while . . . but then it is a choice, so maybe it's not running. I meditate and feel and Be and I find happy again, and sometimes . . . in the oddest moments . . . I get a feeling that is hard to describe other than to say a wave of love washes over me. It happened to me today at work . . . I just had to stop and feel . . . don't know why it hit me but it did . . . so I absorbed and moved on . . . I just chalked it up to someone was thinking loving thoughts of me and somehow I connected . . . it happens every once in a while . . . cool experience . . .

I love who I am (humbly), and I love the world and beauty . . . and I am fine if people cannot understand . . . I am learning that I'd much rather be with me, then with another who is drowning. Loving all the while and being fine that others do not understand me . . . I do not need to explain, and that is freeing in and of itself. We, meaning all of us, were created to be loved, and to not believe that is a lie . . . love starts with our self, because we all have love within us - *the light within all of us* - finding love in ourselves allows for the veil to be lifted allowing us to see the love in others . . . it is a place to grow from pain to inner peace

. . . to know my heart center, to be me . . . and listen to my heart . . . knowing that if I can shift from fear to love would truly be experiencing a miracle . . . or seeing others do the same . . . miracle . . . Love is all around us . . . we either choose to live in love or close our hearts . . . it is a choice made moment to moment . . . heart to heart . . . creating ripple effects . . .

I could go on . . .

I LOVE YOU

This was a quick note to a friend that was having one of those moments we've all experienced . . . overwhelmed and wondering . . . just for a moment . . . the purpose . . . and forgetting how much each of us are loved and are love...

*W*hen the world slows down and the stars dwindle away and your faith is being tested and it feels like a dark day and it all seems like it has been in vain, stop and breathe . . . Feel with your heart that I love you (hug) to the moon and back (hug) and even more deeply and simply (hug) you are in my heart (Hug)...

Love, Love

BEAUTIFUL MESS...

I wept and wept and I wept some more . . . and breathed...
I fell asleep with thoughts running through me about behaviors . . . being human . . . being vulnerable. As I write this, I feel the emotions that take me to the inner edge and take me down into the core . . . where I struggle to sail and navigate . . . through the stormy undercurrent of my feelings. I have a deep sadness that I hold deep within my soul because I was told to always be strong . . . It is a survivor's mantra . . . always dreaming with a patched up heart . . . waking with whisperings . . . "Today may be the day that I can be just me." Then the resisting begins . . . the struggles . . . the questioning . . . telling myself to listen to my heart...

Reflecting on my past is a humbling experience . . . really *seeing* those who intertwined with me, and how much I am like them in so many ways . . . very protective of our hearts, not trusting, clinging, running, lashing out . . . to try to make sense of all that is . . . always searching for the answer that seems just out of reach...

Experiencing what I call the great divide . . . untwining from a beloved is the hardest journey I have made . . . and I am walking through my choice to divorce my husband...

My heart is torn during the last phase of untwining . . . torn because I know it is what I need to do, and taking responsibility for causing so much pain . . . although reflecting back over the past twenty-six years I have always been selfish in the name of compassion . . . I closed my husband out of my heart for the most part . . . I always would try one more time (counseling, therapy, seminars, books, etc.) thinking I could shift his heart to love me for me . . . and all I really was and am doing is being selfish for choosing the slow path . . . justifying my choices as being gentle and kindhearted . . . just selfish and self- absorbed...

I am resisting the experience of the sadness of letting go . . . letting go of what I tried so hard to keep . . . being so controlling in my efforts to try harder . . . trying to prove that I have worth . . . being accepted as I am . . . sharing my heart openly and not being understood caused me so much confusion and pain . . . and the questioning, "What is wrong with me?" Walking around with my heart torn asunder . . . feeling misunderstood . . . like a victim . . . left to pick up the pieces . . . and patch my heart back together . . . to try another day . . . clinging . . .

There is a war between my heart and my mind . . . I know my heart is right . . . I can feel it to my core . . . it is these deep feelings that give me the courage to face each day with the choice of choosing . . . I try my best to listen . . . feel . . . act . . . with my heart...

I am blessed . . . to have walked through my childhood, my marriage, my cancer . . . until I faced my own mortality, I did not quite grasp how sacred each breath and experience is . . . until now . . . there are still days when I pray because of the fear that I will not awake in the morning to experience again . . . because of the weakness I experience in my physical body . . . I am grateful for every morning, every person, and every experience . . . it is a gift I will not ever take for granted . . . even if I am a beautiful mess . . .

TESTIMONIAL - SHE IS LOVE

*I*n the shadowy memories of my youth, I can recall searching for all those lost daydreams of the young lady I was. As I began walking into my womanhood, I slowly let my faith slip away into my past . . . with those distant recollections, I believed in my yesterdays . . . I believed that was where the musings of my heart yearnings belonged.

I allowed myself to get lost in the details of my everyday life . . . living the roles assigned to me by others . . . willingly going along . . . embraced in the hope that by giving what others wanted, I would find what my heart ached for . . . always attempting to perform all the details of everyday living, trying with all my Being to do the right thing, to be acknowledged . . . I wanted to matter as much as they mattered to me . . .

I lost hope, and my faith was stretched so thin, that I became so scared, so tired, and was in so much pain, that it hurt to the core of my soul . . . I fought so long to understand how I gave my heart fully and yet wasn't seen . . . feeling beaten and kicked down . . . I, so gradually, without consciousness, had fallen into ambiguity . . . living in a haze of uncertainty . . . I no longer looked for the beauty and love I saw previously in my life . . . I knew beauty and love were there, but I chose to ignore . . . there was too much pain in expressing my love . . . I longed, too . . . my desire was overwhelming at times...

I didn't listen to my voice . . . I lived in an illusion of lies . . . believing that others where right somehow, which meant I was wrong . . . I lived with rose colored glasses on and with my head in the clouds . . . I chose to walk in the skewed convictions of others . . . my soul slowly washed-out to indistinctiveness . . . and I no longer cared to reach out to connect . . . living through the motions, unwilling to feel . . . because when I felt, showed love, I had to chance the aching and longing of my heart . . . and I was afraid, and feared dreaming too big and going too deep . . .

I understood that I was choosing to live in a lie to protect my fragmented heart . . . the world felt cold to me and I didn't want to seem emotionless anymore because my heart, though sheltered, was not left unaffected. I absorbed each experience and became buried alive with my heart's longings and thoughts . . . always watching, catching glimpses . . . becoming spellbound with the beauty and love or ugliness of the world that I witnessed.

Rarely sharing, I started to climb out slowly, ever so slowly, from the obscurity of my unremarkable, detached days. I knew in my heart I had to be me or die . . . and I did not want to die...

Reaching for anything to hold onto to, I frantically, not wanting to fall back into insignificance, searched . . . through books, school, therapy, seminars . . . searching for my heart answer . . . with each step on my path toward living and practicing unconditional love, I came to understand in fleeting moments and clarity what unconditional love meant . . . freedom, joy, happiness, tenderness, kindness, compassion, sharing, connecting, loving self and all others...

I came to fully understand what tools I have been collecting, but the connection was incomplete between my mind and heart. I had the knowledge . . . I just did not understand how to implement, live, and practice unconditional love. Then it happened . . . I found the key to what I was searching for...

Sharon . . . she saw my heart . . . and I believed her . . . and then I trusted her and leaned in . . . to be embraced in her love. I knew she saw me when she gently spoke the words that quietly brought my heart to opening, in that moment, to feel her love . . . "You are so tender just now."

Those words vibrated inward to my soul and seeped into the seams of my well-guarded patched up heart . . . in that moment, the shift, the softening of my heart, began. I knew to my core I would never be the same . . . no longer stagnant. That inkling of awareness shifted my heart toward walking my path toward love . . . unconditional love . . . Real Love . . .

Sharon cares about my happiness . . . with no thought for herself. She *sees* me . . . she is lovingly straightforward, truthful, authentic . . .

99

teaching with a pure passionate heart . . . allowing me to take baby-steps, and embracing me with love, kindness, tenderness, and compassion . . . to allow me to stumble . . . to grow and learn . . . she makes me feel that I am loved beyond measure and that I matter, am cherished . . . teaching me that when I hold back my heart, I do not allow my love to flow freely.

Sharon shares her wisdom with me about gratefulness, on being a contribution to the world . . . to listen to my voice . . . and that life is a miracle to experience, to find grace, calm, peace in my journey.

Sharon walks humbly in her love light that shines . . . brightly illuminating . . . embracing unconditional love to touch individual's hearts . . . we are blessed because she is a part of our world . . . She is Love...

Love, Love ♥

NATURAL BEAUTY

I wrote this after spending an afternoon with my Real Love Goddess Group . . . .we talked about loving ourselves

E very person in this world with physical form has a natural beauty. There is no one way to be beautiful . . . we can choose to open our eyes with love at any moment to see the exceptionality of every Being. That means accepting our own natural beauty with no judgment, and to see ourselves and others with all the beauty and perfection in our physical body, our dreams, thoughts, hopes, and emotions. By loving all of who we are, and appreciating our rareness, we can find choice in happiness, joy, and love, that goes deeply inward to our Being, and then can burst outward to radiate, shine, sparkle . . . to write the story of our lives with love . . . in every thought, action, emotion, we can chose to walk in love. To build trust and to know self-love will lead to making the right decisions, give us the courage to face issues as they come to us, and know that we individually can embrace the power of love within each of us, and walk humbly the path of loving our inner child . . . and know who we are from the core of our Being. Knowing the power of love is within each of us can help one to find the courage to speak her truth . . . lovingly . . . and to share with all others . . . to create connections, to share in the

100

beauty of the world, both inner and outer. The power of love within each of us gives those who choose to *see* it, the capacity to accept others and self without judgment . . . knowing that when we judge ourselves, we detract from our individualistic beauty . . . and it diminishes our own loveliness, and the gift of sharing it with others.

As we understand and open our hearts to all that love is . . . and know that we are blessed . . . and in knowing this, our gratitude can be renewed and expanded more deeply with each waking moment. That each new day is an opportunity to practice gratefulness for all that we are . . . individually and collectively. In choosing to unconditionally love ourselves in our natural beauty, we are choosing to love all others in kindness, compassion, tenderness, joy, happiness, and love.

Know that to me, each of you, and all others, are exceptionally beautiful . . . and I am blessed to share in connecting in the presence of love and true beauty. I am Blessed.

Love, Love

GOOD NIGHT WITH LOVE

oday I just wanted to be . . . no decisions . . . no judgments . . . no feelings . . . it was not to be...

Feeling like going inward and going on auto pilot . . . but I can't quite get there because I now know in my heart that this is the absolutely wrong thing to do . . . and I do want to feel everything and let it flow through me . . . which means not tuning out (running) but rather experiencing . . . I have to be all in or not in at all . . . so I'm in . . . But today I very much did not want to be . . . I am happy to have my day come to a close . . . It was one of those retrospective days . . . with so much to absorb . . . I am walking through grief and pain . . . shifting to a new experience in life . . . it feels surreal . . . going over my day and sitting here feeling . . . I realized, once again, that I forgot to ask for the one thing I want and need the most . . . that is to be held, embraced . . . I seem to forget or become afraid . . . and do not speak my truth (needs/wants) when I speak to people . . . I feel so tender just now . . . and I am not use to letting that bubble up at this level . . . I, in the past, rarely allowed for the tenderness tangled with pain to come to surface . . . My focus was always purposely distracted, now though I am not distracted . . . that is where I am just now . . . Good night, with love, ♥

ME

*T*he past few days have been so emotional . . . one minute I am feeling happy, and then like today, when driving to my new home, I began to cry . . . it is so weird not going home to the place where my daughter is . . . I am going to miss her presence. I know she is never home, and we will be together more with me not being there, but it is a weird sensation not to be able to walk into her room or smell her . . . or hug or smile at her everyday . . .

Yesterday I was feeling overwhelmed and very sick to my stomach . . . I am trying to take this one moment at a time . . . breathing . . . I am trying not to shut down to deal . . . I just feel like curling up in a ball and disappearing for a while . . . I feel like I am living in slow motion . . . and just taking stuff as it comes . . . grieving my previous life but knowing that I would be miserable if had I stayed . . . He and I are just too different in our views of the world and people . . . this truly will be a shift that will stretch my boundaries . . . I hope I am capable enough to handle this . . . not sure . . . willing to try though . . .

I keep reminding myself that there is nothing to fear . . . I am loved . . . (list people who love me) that I have everything I need and everything to be grateful for . . . at least I have a new day, every day, to make choices . . . and that in itself makes me feel blessed.. .because I know I am . . . .

"I WILL STOP THE WORLD FOR YOU..."

*T*hese words were spoken to another as I sat in group and listened to the interchange between the wise person and the person sharing . . . This phrase is so personal for me, I realized as I took it in and internalized . . . I knew just then these are the words I always wanted to have my parents and Him say to me, "You matter and you are worth stopping the world for." Such a simple turn of phrase that has such an impact when spoken to another . . . Then I remembered these are lyrics to a song I connected to when I was growing up...

When I was a child/young lady, I learned the songs that I loved to hear, like Rainbow Connection or Wonderful World, or I am a Child of God, and You Are So Beautiful to Me and I'd sing to myself and I would believe what I heard . . . with my whole heart and soul . . . I knew if I kept trying and looking I would find *it* although as a little girl I did not know what *it* was . . . but when I heard those songs it made me feel embraced in tenderness for those few moments . . . *it* became my focus, my purpose . . . I stopped the world long enough to feel *it* when I listened to music as a child/ young lady . . . running to daydreams of what little girls/young ladies dream about...

Then I stopped . . . I didn't listen because I did not want to connect and feel anymore (victim) . . . I was always being told I was wrong to feel the way I felt or that I had my head in the clouds . . . or I was delusional for *seeing* the world the way I do . . . I only shared with a select few . . . like my children . . . mostly my children . . . I wanted to show them how beautiful the world is . . . I was very guarded and I did not want my heart touched or judged . . . for oh so long my soul was so depleted . . . and I would give in sometimes and the melody and lyrics would touch me and I would turn my back on my heart . . . believing I should not stop the world for me . . . I believed the lie . . . and I kept running...

And running . . . hiding (clinging to the lie). I knew I would have to reconnect and feel again . . . to explore all those feelings that I said were not important enough to stop the world for . . . I knew I was lying and I had to choose to live in my illusion or take a leap of faith, lean in, trust, and have enough courage to practice love openly, sharing . . . and in sharing, I mean being vulnerable. As I stumble through my vulnerability, I feel the shifting of my heart and the walls that where made of brick and steel feel so paper thin. I can feel and see beyond the walls, with more glimpses of clarity as the walls crumble away to mere rubble to step over and continue on my path . . . Because I know from the core of Being that we ALL matter and that WE are ALL worth stopping the world for . . . and that includes me...

MOMENTS LEAST EXPECTED

*S*ilently lying in bed, listening to the soft patter of the rain fall from the eaves of the rooftop onto the hard cement ground just outside the cracked window of my bedroom, unable to drift off to sleep, I go inward . . . and my thoughts course to reminiscences that only seem to come up in those moments least expected . . . I am overwhelmed with mixed emotions. Tears start to stream down my quite, silent face . . . as whisperings of voices of those who have journeyed my path with me . . . sharing expressions remembered, sometimes so tender, loving . . . sometimes callous and uncaring . . . In my awareness, I can go back to those memories and feel in my heart . . . the love or pain I experienced in those moments . . . stepping through the shroud of protection that guards well, even to this day, the darkness I walked through, and I am absorbed into my former self . . . to re-experience with the woman's understanding I have today . . . to comfort the little girl/young lady forever locked into the chasm of the murkiest corners of my heart . . . to draw from and learn and grow from . . . so I look and see and try to understand . . . absorb and to love my former self in those memories . . .

I dug my way out so many times, and each stretch of working harder to conceal what my heart wanted to reveal . . . but felt out of place . . . misconstrued . . . always second guessing . . . my heart always whispered to me that I am perfect the way I am, but I chose to believe the lies for so long . . . it was easier, safer to play the martyr and suffer and look outward and stay focused on running and not looking inward, always tuning my voice out, fully conscious of the destruction I was causing myself . . . I told myself I didn't care. I knew the moment I uttered those words out loud for the first time . . . that it was a lie . . . I knew from the core of me that it was a lie . . . and I did care . . . immensely. I spent many, many years trying to convince myself that I did not care . . . instead, I lived in a world of fear . . . never forgetting who I am . . . always dreaming of better days . . . realizing that I let so much slip by . . . and telling the truth in whispers . . . and causing so much pain in the truth because of living in panic that I would be discovered...

That I am a daydreamer . . . who feels deeply . . . and loves to wear my heart on my sleeve . . . and being sensitive . . . showing compassion, tenderness, kindness, love . . . whenever possible . . . it is who I am . . . a dream weaver . . . who imagines I want to share, and embracing visions as discovered . . . to find the possibilities . . . those are the dreams I want to walk into as I drift into my nightly slumber...

Love, Love ♥

LONELINESS

I woke this morning feeling incomplete . . . not in the right frame of mind . . . I sat with the feeling as I drove to work . . . wondering what it was . . . then slowly, as I just let my feelings bubble up, I recognized the feeling as loneliness . . . not actual being alone . . . but the feeling of aloneness even when interacting with others . . . but somehow disconnected...walking in a haze. This feeling is the feeling I always ran from all my life . . . wrapping myself in activities and other people's lives (fixing...aka controlling) so I would not have to *see* or give attention to myself (running). All my life I was afraid to stop and look and feel because if I would see and feel, I then would have a knowing, an understanding, and then I would have the responsibility to choose differently. Choosing differently meant giving up the safety and praise that I worked so diligently to obtain and collect through my behaviors...

The controlling kept me from feeling love, because I was too busy being focused on myself and my needs . . . in the disguise of professing my good deeds for others . . . never taking a moment to breathe . . . and feel . . . that was dangerous . . . I avoided that at all costs...

The separation from the individuals that I traded so heavily with, has given me some insight into how deep into controlling and clinging I was. I can see that I was manipulating . . . and always trying to figure out the next move . . . to stay one step ahead (controlling) to earn my praise and safety (clinging). Just now I am having this thought . . . that I was in fear and running from my feelings, and ignoring my voice, because when

I had those moments of clarity as to how I really felt inwards, I became scared (losing safety and praise) of what that meant . . . and I did not have the courage to speak my truth (victim).

Just typing this is hard . . . sharing this is even harder . . . it's where I am coming from, and I can see that . . . I have such a fear of being judged and labeled . . . and that is hard to share . . . being open and vulnerable is so messy for me (trying to control) . . . and crying in front of people (being vulnerable) is hard . . . it comes back to being judged . . . by myself mostly . . . which in turn leads to feeding my feeling of loneliness (being a victim).

I have faith though . . . and I believe in me . . . I believe in love . . . that I am loved . . . I am grateful for all that was and is in my life . . . I am humbled by all of you and the openness and love that is shared with me and the love I witness shared with others . . . we are blessed.

Love, Love

THE DANCE

I wrote this about my perception of co-dependency . . .

On and on the fragile dance went . . . continuously, from one dance partner to the next . . . silently gliding on the dance floor which felt like eggshells beneath my feet . . . ever conscious of every step taken . . . to not make a mistake...although outwardly, my partners looked graceful, and beautiful, in leading the dance . . . I could feel the tension that flowed between us . . . the vibration of my partners dancing with me. Intertwining in the intricate steps, taught me so gradually, that it felt effortless to dance the dance . . . that always before seemed to create fear, distress, confusion, inner turmoil, and chaos...

So indirect was the action, but so direct in the soundless communication . . . that I could feel within to the core of my soul . . . we danced so flowingly, smoothly, looking so elegantly, as we mislead the observers into believing the story we presented. It was so deceptive to those who looked on, not understanding the concealed grasp I was in . . . willingly being led, controlled, from the measurable pressure applied to those most sensitive parts of me . . . that I could only feel . . . my mask always on with the smile I was taught to wear . . . never making eye contact with others who twirled by us . . . I did not want to break the rhythm . . . always being diligent not to have a misstep . . .

The dance was so intimate . . . so settling, easy . . . that I became mesmerized by the words whispered softly into my ear . . . "You're too sensitive, you're crazy, you're imagining things," or, "I never said that..." The words spoken so quietly . . . it did not feel real . . . and I was unsure . . . and when I questioned, the dance became so intense that I felt like a captive performer within the arms of my partner, and I could not escape . . . I could only conform to the dance I was taught to dance . . . even when the steps I was swaying into felt somehow wrong, not quite on mark, with what I was feeling to be right and true . . . Always questioning my ability to learn my own dance . . . resigning myself to the fate I had created . . . that I did not know the dance steps . . . and I could not quite get the steps in the right order to please . . . and to be the perfect dance partner that was needed by others...

I knew the dance steps well enough to move . . . to distract my partner into moving back into our familiar deliberate dance, performing . . . I became accustomed to dancing without feeling . . . letting my partner stand in the center and I in the shadows . . . the role of the follower assigned to me felt safe . . . all the while, wondering why I could not step from follower to lead, leaving the shadows of the dance floor and coming to center . . . understanding somehow that this is where I should be, but not understanding how to find a new dance to dance to.

I became at ease on the cold dark dance floor as I weaved in and out of the set music played for me . . . going inward and trying to remember why I started to dance to begin with . . . and being so comfortable and unaware of the dance I chose . . . to continue the dance of co-dependency . . . always pleasing, fixing, controlling. Letting my partner, in this elaborate dance, lead, defining the dance I should dance . . . instead of choosing the dance of my own soul.

Little by little I found the courage to question the dance I was participating in . . . listening to my heart . . . whisperings of the song my heart wants to dance in. I am untwining from the desperate grasp of the co-dependent dance . . . I am attempting to move gracefully off the dance

107

floor . . . to practice dancing spontaneously to my own heart song . . . to live my dream out loud . . . moving from the fragile dance of co-dependency to the delicate dance of finding me . . . I'm learning the freedom of leaping, spinning, twirling, finding my inner rhythm and drifting onto a new dance floor . . . my daydreams coming to reality . . . the music feels right . . . and I can dance freely in the song of joy, happiness, love . . . giving and receiving, compassion, kindness, tenderness . . . that is the dance I want to practice dancing . . . every day, every moment . . . I have been blessed . . . and given more time to find my heart song and dance . . . and the opportunity to practice dancing with others . . . who can share in my heart song and dance with me . . . and that is what truly matters to me . . . dancing and sharing with others...

JUDGMENTS

*J*udgment is really a pattern of self-destruction, a most unloving action I seem to continually practice on myself when feeling less-than (victim) . . . believing the lies or not believing the truths shared with me . . . (lying to myself/victim) there were and are people who express to me, how worthy and loved I was and am, but I did and do not believe them when I get lost in my mind . . . instead of listening to the whispering of truths that reside in my heart . . . I have a deep-seated fear that if I share my heart, I will be judged and or not accepted again. This scares me to silence . . . even now I find myself reliving that fear . . . in my moments of self-doubt . . .

As I am growing into my true self, I am able to understand that others judgments do not have to be accepted by me . . . although I still catch myself agreeing with others about their judgments of me . . . whether I agree with the judgment or not . . . in order not to create a conflict, or I catch myself minimizing my worth, and or my life, and or how loved I am . . . I know the fear stems from attempting to speak my truth . . . so I learned to keep my thoughts to myself unless asked . . . was given permission to speak . . . I am so used to being told I am wrong to speak . . . or if I did speak, my voice, my feelings, were discounted . . . So I just stopped and started to fade away . . . never having anything to share . . . because my heart believed that I was less-than, that I did not matter . . . I logically understood that to be a lie, but my heart did not quite believe it . . . until fairly recently...

Oui, just typing that . . . sharing that truth and seeing that in print about me . . . makes me cringe...

It is so easy to fall back into my comfortableness (running) if I am not being aware . . . and let someone else decide my worth . . . letting myself fade into the emptiness and numbness . . . of being a victim. Not taking responsibility . . . instead of taking the time to see/feel/ understand my own self-worth (fear of speaking my truth/lying). These actions and neglect of myself, fed and feeds my insecurity, creating doubt (victim) . . . It is a habit, to repeat the words of negativity (lying), believing them, as if the words were a truth instead of the lies that they are...

I am seeing that I easily justified my judgments of myself and others . . . it is really very irresponsible, blaming others . . . and giving my power away to others . . . I seek acceptance externally, instead of owning my feelings . . . and knowing from within my true self-worth . . .

Instead embracing the gift of an experience or mistake, I used the information as ammunition to shoot holes in my self-worth, to prove that "they" were always right about me . . . then, I would try even harder to seek approval . . . and double up my effort to prove my self-worth . . . that I was good enough . . . and every once in a while . . . I would get that confirmation (praise/power/safety) that would reinforce the feeling of what I thought was "approval" . . . but that is external, and that feeling fades quite quickly, and it took more effort to get the same level of feeling the next time . . . it is a vicious cycle that wore me down physically, mentally, spiritually . . .

The energy I feed into the judgments has created some insights for me . . . not willing to feed that draining energy source . . . when I look at my judgments, I can see the behaviors I reinforce, lying, self-attacking, victim, clinging, running . . . all are intertwined and feed each other . . . staying locked in the cycle of repeating the same behaviors . . . releasing the hard earned judgments means setting myself free from the draining of my life energy . . . creating responsibility for my own happiness . . . and not looking externally for my worth . . . coming to awareness that I do not have to give up anything to be me or to feel love . . . I also have come to understand that all the resistance I have had in acknowledging my part in these feelings, has only strengthen those feelings . . . I am now ready to *see* those feelings . . . and acknowledge and know that they are not right or wrong, good or bad, but just feelings and thoughts to acknowledge . . . and let it be . . . to flow . . . through me.

It is a process for me . . . opening my heart,

having the courage to be vulnerable...

courage to be human . . . courage to just be me . . .

MOVING INTO MYSELF

J just wanted to share with you the feelings I am having . . . as I move into myself and be *me* naturally . . . I seem to attract people who cannot hear me, even when I am direct with them . . . and I become afraid, because it brings me back to not feeling safe. I was thinking about safety and how I looked for it from a very young age . . . it was my highest priority . . . I realized, that was why I dated my boyfriend in high school for three years . . . so I could tell people that I had a boyfriend, and I was unavailable . . . He cheated on me . . . ignored me . . . and got frustrated with me because I would not have sex with him . . . looking back, I see now, that I used him . . . although I tried to convince myself that I cared for him . . . I knew within two dates that I would never ever be intertwined with him . . . but he was safe . . . and I was kind to him . . . and he was someone to see once a week . . . we did not go to the same school . . . shortly after I broke it off with him, I realized I was not being honest with him, and I knew I would never intertwine with him . . . (Physically, spiritually, mentally)

Then I became afraid again, when I had this guy from my church stalking me and other girls . . . I would pull my curtain back, and he would be there . . . or I would go to work and he would be there in the distance . . . it was so freaky and scary . . . and I clung to the first guy who did not treat me like such an object . . . HIM . . . I clung to him . . . although I thought I loved him . . . and I grew to love him on some level . . . but I can see clearly now how scared I was . . . willing to trade *me* for safety . . . because I did not know how to protect myself...

Even when I dated and married him, he was my safety . . . when people would be inappropriate with me or cling to me, and they could not hear me when I was direct with them . . . he would step in and somehow those people would hear him . . . I spoke my truth, but too softly . . . fearing that I would

110

hurt people's feelings . . . all the while scared of them . . . feeling like an object to those people instead of *seeing* me . . .

I hope that makes sense...

I am experiencing those feelings again . . . they are coming up and I know I am over-reacting but . . . I keep repeating to myself that I am safe . . . and there is nothing to fear . . . but on a cellular level, I have not absorbed that truth into my being . . . only on the surface . . .

I am still working on trying to be firm in my voice and not backing down . . . but the truth of the matter is I am afraid of being attacked again. Physically and verbally, that seems to be the reaction I get when I am firm . . . so I start caretaking about how the person might hear me . . . and trying to control . . . because I do not know how to say it quite directly without feeling like I was being a little bit to mean . . . I need to learn this skill and soon . . . I am seeing this will be the people I will attract over and over until I can learn how to set my boundaries clearly, without hesitation . . . this is about me *seeing* me . . . and walking through my fear . . . and listening to my inner voice when my body signaling to me that something is not quite right . . . then I go into questioning myself . . . it does not really matter if the threat is real or not . . . it is real to me . . . and that is enough reason to listen to my voice, even if not totally accurate . . .

Love, Love

YOU

I wrote this to a friend . . . my feelings . . . trying to express...

I know I am walking through many emotions and I have to give careful consideration to what I am feeling. I have to trust that events will unfold the way events need to happen, and I have the responsibility, choice, as to how to accept and perceive events. I do not worry about much, and I have a great amount of faith . . . in this world there is little room for worry, but a lot of room for positive action . . . to tap into this ability to consciously choose to see the truth and beauty . . . the ability to do good whenever possible, to our best capability . . . and to contribute to the meaning of life . . . I have also learned that I can help

111

create that loving flow when I give free reign to what is the best in me, what expresses my rareness...

I guess what I am saying . . . whatever it is that you are walking through . . . I love you . . . when I say, "I love you," I am not talking about the things you do for me . . . although appreciated, is not why I love you . . . I love you for just Being . . . the best way to describe it, is like when I look at my children, and am in their presence . . . love swells within . . . no matter what event is going on in their lives . . . them just Being . . . makes my heart shine brilliantly . . . sounds mushy . . . hard to describe . . . but I know from the core of me that this feeling is eternal . . . I feel blessed and am so appreciative to feel at this level . . . just know that if you need a friend, sister, or whatever, I will be here . . . stumbling through my words . . . to express my truth . . . I seem to use so many words . . . to express my feelings...

May peace be with you...

MY TRUTH

I have found comfort, safety in enfolding myself in the familiarity of my skewed beliefs of how I appear to the outside world, and I measure my worth by those inward evaluations, my beliefs about myself...

Everything that I thought defined me, are just identities, that I have become attached to . . . my true self observing my life . . . watching and absorbing and waiting for something...

Vulnerable and uncomfortable . . . shedding the beliefs I have accumulated, unconsciously identifying who I had become but am no more, a wife, a part of a couple, a daughter who felt responsible for her mom's happiness, a mommy, always busy and lost in the details of raising three beautiful, amazing children, always wrapped up in so many activities, neglecting myself. And those few moments I could've used for myself, I used to give to others, actually finding ways to run from what I knew was the truth for me . . . that I was not being truly me . . .

And now losing those identities and trying to walk around with the awkwardness of being *me* instead of being part of a *we* is so dreamlike

112

for me . . . it does not quite feel real . . . coming to myself . . . unraveling from my co-dependency . . . that is so clear to me now . . . looking back . . . *seeing* or actually remembering my true self (soul) speaking softly to me of my truths. I would look and feel and purposely turn my head gently away, whispering inward, "Not yet, not now."

I am recognizing that I am not my circumstances . . . I am still me inside . . .

I am not what I choose to do . . . I will still be inside of me...

I am not the roles accepted by me . . . I have a lot of roles, but none completely define who I am, only what I do...

As I grow and change, so do my current views and connections, expanding and evolving, creating new possibilities . . . finding the courage to bring to surface the true person I am . . . To be authentic, truthful, genuinely me...

So . . . Who Am I? My true nature . . . What are the truisms . . . that I have seen in me?

I love to play, have fun, laugh . . . I find joy in dancing, I love dancing . . . I love music, people, connecting and sharing...

BUT . . .

I also become insecure in the blink of an eye when reminded of who I should be instead of remembering who I am . . . that connecting, sharing with others causes me fear . . . that I have to build my courage to walk through the uneasiness again and again . . . to be able to feel comfortable in being open and vulnerable . . . each time, I am finding the love and acceptance of walking through the self-created haze of fear, and the fog is not so dense and seems to dissipates within a short amount of time . . . instead of always feeling like an eternal mist . . . the sunshine breaks through . . . warming me inwards and I can *see* glimpses of the real me...

MY TRUTH...

That I am vivacious, passionate, enthusiastic, effervescence, imaginative, perceptive . . . that I LOVE PEOPLE, that we are here to teach and learn with each other . . . that love is all that really matters. I believe in the softening of hearts, connecting with and loving our inner-selves, finding our innocence, is an everyday miracle that I get to experience . . . shifting, growing, learning, and sharing. I believe in, and try to practice, compassion, tenderness, kindness . . . because it matters to me . . . that every person is worth stopping the world for (I really love that) . . . because we are all just part of each other . . . connecting . . . ebbing and flowing . . . creating ripple effects that cause waves of gratitude in me, helping me to understand the abundance of love that there is, and coming to understand how truly blessed I am . . . and loved beyond measure . . . I almost forgot . . . I believe in Angels . . . And that is me just now . . . *Love, Love* ♥

MAGIC

Exploring me...

*C*onnecting to the magic that is me, is a walk towards identifying and growing into consciousness of my inner resistance . . . of bringing to surface the genuine, authentic, true self . . . always curious, I find myself stopping to find a deeper awareness to my self-opposition . . . and try to discover, grow, ascertain, and learn to release and find the freedom of trusting my intuitive, natural self . . . this yielding, softening, relaxing, allows for my feelings to flow . . . to the truth that I know to be true . . . That I am love, we are all the source of love, that I am safe, that I am precious, that I am on a journey of personal growth to move out of the darkness created by my ego to protect me . . . that no longer serves a productive purpose . . . It is so easy to get tangled in the details, analyzing, running from what is right there in our choices . . . That I can reach for the light (love) understanding this is where I am naturally drawn, to the healing . . . this requires me to show myself, with all my wounds, resisting the ego (fear) to hide . . . if I choose to hide, then I do not grow . . . the ego is so familiar that the discomfort is barely noticeable on the conscious level . . . but in those quite moments, when being retrospective . . . the bubbling begins . . . my natural self-wanting to come to surface . . . and be healed and play and live in joy and love . . . when finding, connecting to the magic in me...

MAKING OUR OWN CHOICES

I have learned over time that we cannot choose for people how they will perceive the events and experiences that are theirs to walk through. When we start trying to control (fix) other's experiences, we take their ability to choose and take responsibility for their choices, and stunt their growth toward living an authentic life. When we make our own choices, we gain a sense of responsibility. We begin to feel a sense of freedom and confidence in ourselves . . . which gives us the courage to start having faith in ourselves . . . to see the many choices we really do have. Self-acceptance will then develop into a healthy love for self which gives the individual the capacity to love self and others with compassion. I have found that I can love a person in their choices and have compassion as they choose the path they are willing to walk . . . really there is no wrong way to live our life . . . the experience we have is based in our choices so at any moment we can choose differently . . . change our perspective and release ourselves from the lies we tell ourselves . . . About how life happens to us, when in reality, we are making choices in every moment . . . we have the ability to choose differently how we see life, the experiences, people, and ourselves. This I know . . . we are all worthy, love, and have a path to walk. We are here to teach and learn with each other . . . and to be unconditionally loving . . . and coming to awareness of this purpose can make the details of our lives seem insignificant . . . as we understand from our Being . . . that we all matter, and we always have a choice as to how we experience our lives . . . at the end of the day, it is about the connections (love) we share with each other . . . we get to choose how we see those connections....

SET FREE

I wrote this after having lunch with my soon to be ex-husband, and coming to terms with our life together...

I know I'm bound to be set free if I listen to my heart . . . learning to take care of myself by being silent . . . heeding within . . . to choose my next step, and raise my hopeful influence of words to share with others . . . I have the choice . . . to absorb and feel and learn. The more I learn, the more I want to know and share . . . seeing the beauty, loveliness, in myself and all others . . . and sharing my feelings . . . ebbing and flowing as I find my footing . . . creating a resilient base to stand on . . . to take leaps of faith . . . believing from the core of me . . . I am on the right path . . . learning to be gentle with myself, no expectations, just experiencing as I make choices, and accepting . . . So much easier than trying to control, it takes the stress away . . . at least that is how it feels . . . freeing in making choices.

With that being said . . . I still get unsure about *me* sometimes . . . usually when people are expecting so much from me . . . and . . . I am not going to think about it . . . because I know what I want to share needs to be heard . . . it feels right to me...

Also...

Met with him and we came to a settlement. The lawyer emailed me back and she will be putting the divorce decree together . . . The lunch, at a restaurant, was so, I don't know, but he shared his thoughts about me . . . I just listened and tried to re-direct conversation back to what we were there to do . . . He is resigned, I guess, to this divorce . . . I just let him talk for a while, I smiled at him, and thought to myself, He does not *see* me . . . still about what I can or can't do, instead of who I am . . . Mmm . . . that is okay though . . . I am good with that . . . it (our twining) is almost untwined . . .

My thoughts just now . . . I jumped, and I *knew* I would fly instead of fall . . . and instead of running away from me . . . I stayed . . . even though I was not sure if I truly had it in me sometimes . . . I wanted to and want to give it (love) my all (surrender) . . . because in giving and leaning in, I knew and know that this is the only way I will know me . . . believing and seeing the truth . . . that WE ALL ARE LOVE . . . and when a person comes to this awareness the choice of responsibility is there to continue to grow and expand, to share, learn and teach . . . one person at a time, ripple effects . . . Even when I think I can't . . . I feel within me that I can...

I have chosen Love and I will not pause my heart to question (think) . . . instead, when I let love flow freely, I will completely let go of my fears . . . stirrings . . . listening . . . with grace in my heart...

I feel lovely just the way I am . . . just now...

NOTEBOOK

This day was hard . . . for a moment . . . I lost my notebook that I wrote in with about a year's worth of ideas, thoughts, feelings . . . more importantly, I lost the pictures of my children that I carried in that notebook . . . I was truly bummed for a few hours and then realized that this is an opportunity to stretch and grow my faith in my writing . . . myself . . . and just go with the flow...

S o . . . for those who don't know me personally, I tend to be a little scatter-brained at times . . . it is something I am working on taming . . . my thoughts, imagination will start going into overdrive, playing with words and expressing my feelings around a word or phrase, and I tend to get lost in thought . . . works well for writing but not so much for the day to day tasks I need to complete . . . for instance . . . this past weekend, I misplaced my notebook that I carry with me to jot down thoughts, words, phrases, quotes to go back to later to explore my feelings around a certain word/s . . . I have uncompleted writings that I wanted to explore more in depth . . . not having the notebook also gives me a new fresh beginning . . . to maybe formulate a better way to go about being inspired . . . letting go of the old and opening to new possibilities and opening to new opportunities . . . to experience a new day, everyday . . . To have the gift of choice to direct my life and choose to see beauty, love in me and others and know we are one . . . that I get to choose to practice kindness, tenderness, compassion, and witness small everyday miracles . . . that I have the choice to share my heart . . . and in sharing I experience connection with other's hearts . . . learning and teaching . . . expanding . . . creating ripple effects that will move beyond . . . to love and including all others . . . one person at a time . . . Being . . . embraced in oneness . . . I could go on...

Love, Love

No Need to Explain

I wrote this after interactions with people, and my perception of how I felt it went . . . I was acting like a victim . . . and that is okay . . . Because that is where I was when I wrote this...

*T*his is a lonely life sometimes . . . trying to stretch and I am wondering why I am doing this . . . continually being given information from others . . . I feel as though I am not *seen* . . . and I do not know how to do this because I feel like there is something people are looking for, the right answer, or maybe how to "fix" me . . . and when I share person to person, I seem to be stopped in mid-sentence or thought . . . because I am not talking continually and pausing to feel . . . writing is easier to share and stay in touch with my true feelings . . . instead of being directed with questions to a different thought flow . . . cutting off what I wanted to share and getting caught up in the details of the direction of the conversation . . .

There are some things I have learned, and talking, explaining, my heart to others can be difficult . . . the conversations feel more to me about the person listening and wanting to "fix" and not about hearing, accepting me . . . and there is a disconnect . . . There are times when I feel very much surrounded by love . . . then there are times when I open up to share and then feel judged and not *seen* . . . then that is about me really . . . I am working on that . . . being okay . . . when it is obvious I am not *seen* . . . it is what it is . . . I know that most people are well intentioned . . . and want the best for me . . . so I just smile and say, "Thank you for sharing," or, "I need to ponder that," and I close my eyes and whisper inward, "Let it be, let it go..." understanding my worth to my core . . . no need to explain . . .

Retro Perspective

Feeling can be so darn confusing sometimes...

I want to just be . . . I become very retrospective, and absorb and feel deeply . . . maybe too deeply . . . disconnecting from the ego .

. . and observing...Listening . . . I learn (feel) so much . . . I do not know how to explain these feelings that I feel so deeply . . . I know you are one of the few that "gets" me when I use the words that people attach a different meaning to . . . and I do not know how to express accurately or clearly and then I am not heard or seen . . . I am working on how to express my feelings clearly to be understood . . . I do not know if that is even possible . . . to describe these feelings . . . without sounding like a Pollyanna, or like having my head in the clouds . . . I *see* the reality of life and people . . . I love and have more compassion with each new experience . . . I want to express clearly . . . and then I don't . . . I believe that each encounter with others is a gift and was meant to be . . . I do not question . . . instead . . . stop, look, listen, feel, and act . . . I have had in the past few months some amazing encounters with people who have drifted into my life . . . I have been blessed and my life enriched because of these encounters . . . it was meant to be . . . either to teach or learn . . . to experience . . .

I expressed that I was angry yesterday . . . I thought about that for a while . . . I am not angry with him . . . I am angry . . . well not raging angry . . . more like disappointed in myself, and how I have interacted with him. I have been less then loving or compassionate with him . . . and see every action as a potential "attack" from him . . . so very unkind of me . . . I do not want to have these feelings with him, he deserves better than that . . . I do not have that capacity to be that way . . . with him . . . just yet . . . I truly want the best for him . . . and I see him trying, in his own way, to make better choices . . . this will be such a struggle within him . . . and he ultimately will have to be responsible for his choices . . . and the same for me . . . even if he perceives me causing him pain . . .

Just now, though . . . I want to be held and told I am fine . . . just the way I am . . . I know this to be true . . . but today I am questioning . . . and thoughts run through my head . . . what is my purpose and can I really make a difference? Or should I just step away . . . not be vulnerable . . . then I would go numb again . . . I do not like to be numb . . . I want to be connected . . . I truly do love people . . . all people . . . even if I cannot express my feelings accurately . . . I know my worth and all others worth . . . we, after all, are one in the same and are connected, and there is universal love, and deep connecting love, when we stop, look, listen to our hearts . . . and choose to act or not to act . . . I guess that is my purpose . . . our purpose . . . connecting and loving . . . Love, Love

MASTERPIECE

Sometimes waves of love just "hit" me . . . and I just want to share . . . and this is the space I was in when I wrote this...

$\mathcal{I}$ have whispered prayers, wished upon stars, and hoped with all my Being (heart) that each person connected to me will know what a blessing each of you are in my life . . . and know how exceptional, enduring, and unique you are to me . . . I am grateful you have a presence in my life . . . and have a place in my heart . . . You are a masterpiece . . . Never forget what a treasure you are . . . you are something . . . and someone . . . You are uniquely, one-of-a-kind . . . You were meant to shine . . . Sharing, spreading your light everywhere . . . you can and do make a beautiful contribution to this world . . . You are love and are loved beyond measure . . . Peace and joy to you...

Love, Love

UNSOLICITED QUESTIONS

For some reason, I have a very hard time with being too curious and giving advice . . . or passing judgment through questions that were not solicited . . . I am learning it is better to just listen . . . sometimes I do not need to have the answers because the answers have nothing to do with me . . . sometimes people just want to be heard . . . I know I do . . . so I am practicing being mindful . . . I want to connect to others with love . . . and that is what matters . . . not answers, fixing, controlling, manipulating . . . just let go . . .

$\mathcal{U}$ nsolicited questions or advice is a form of trying to fix . . . control (attacking) . . . Trying to manipulate, change the outcome, controlling choices because of being afraid, in fear of not being loved . . . So selfish, and unloving on my part . . . I was not truly listening . . . and

120

only thinking of myself . . . I see that clearly . . . I will strive to be mindful of my reactions (feelings) . . .

Love Love

WINDS OF FREEDOM

I'm trying to unravel and listen to my heart instead of my mind . . . I am believing on such a deep level that I don't quite measure up . . . attacking myself with lies, and believing the lies at some subtle level, and walking into victimhood . . . processing and seeing that clearly just now . . . when my heart (spirit) tells me otherwise . . . that I am love and my presence here does matter . . . That I can contribute . . .

This is hard for me to share because of believing no one wants to hear what I want to share . . . And fear of being judged . . . which I internalize as being wrong somehow . . . accepting judgments of others as my truths . . . Good and not the so good . . . I'm seeing and rebuilding and beginning to have the awareness of my worth . . . Each person's worth . . .

Breathing . . .

$\mathcal{F}$eelings are coursing through me, sporadically catching my attention between my daily tasks of living in the world . . . sometimes so distracted, like now, at work, I have to stop and listen, feel, and let the words flow from me to share . . . sometimes sharing those intimate, precious, vulnerable emotional states can leave me feeling so completely visible to myself . . . that I cannot discount the truth in my awareness of those moments of clarity . . . it stretches my heart to expand and becomes even deeper and more expansive than I ever thought possible . . .

I do not know how to describe accurately, as the words that come to me just don't seem to impart the feelings I am experiencing in moments of stillness . . . the energy that flows through me, like in a trance state, but still aware enough . . . to perform those daily tasks . . . the undercurrent of energy is felt at a deeper level (spiritual) while bobbing at the surface (physical) searching for those moments in my day to connect, even if for a moment, to feel deeply within that energy . . .

then the moment is there . . . in the twinkling of an eye, like now, and I am riding on the winds of what I can only describe as freedom . . . freedom to soar and feel deeply . . . and in flashes, joining in the universal harmony . . . feeling the energy of love gracefully, reverently, coursing through me . . . us . . . surfacing within my physical being . . . tears of gratitude, love, connectedness, humbled and touched . . . and my thoughts (feelings) wander in those instants to all that share their love with me . . . and knowing I am loved beyond measure and that I matter . . . And my soul, feels surrounded in all that is . . . love . . . and in those moments my heart expands and wants to connect to all to share these moments . . .

that is me just now . . .

Love, Love

ME JUST NOW...

I was having one of those days when I wrote this about my purpose . . . yet again questioning my worth...and believing that I cannot make a difference...then remembering who I am...it always come to self . . . love . . . giving and receiving...

*J*ourneying along in my life . . . creating connections . . . questions keep seeping into my awareness, created by my lower self, ego, questioning myself . . . is there a reason to try? Feeling ill in moments at the thought of maybe not finding, living my purpose, speaking my voice . . . questioning why I have this deep sensation of moving forward, in persistence . . . to share what I know to be my Truths . . . the urge is overwhelming . . . and in those moments my mind (ego) says STOP . . . and my heart (spirit) says KEEP GOING . . . and yet I seem to tilt towards giving up . . . with contemplations of . . . Is it all just out of reach? Can I truly make a difference? Is my purpose already served, and I just do not *see*? Then, that is another illusion (lie) I buy into . . . in those moments of self-doubt . . . creeping into my conscious thoughts . . . loosely twined together creating misconceptions (lies) . . . and I seem to absorb those mistaken beliefs as my truths . . . adding yet another layer to travel through . . . on my path of finding me . . . obstructing my footpath with untruths, of details that belong to others . . . not quite listening, believing, the truths that speak very clearly to me . . . from deep within . . . realizing when I close my eyes I can create (feel) the love and acceptance I crave so deeply sometimes . . . that love and acceptance is within me . . . I forget sometimes, as this is a new belief system to me . . . to be consciously walking and embracing as my own, always knowing within me . . . and all others . . . that love is shining from within each of us . . . even if I, and others, cannot, in moments, be aware of this TRUTH. Understanding, seeing, feeling, the tenderness, love, compassion . . . knowing that where I contribute my love is the way I will feel, live my life . . . my heart will trump my mind, even if I stumble and forget . . . the Truths I know to be true . . . I do know that each of us are here with a purpose, our presence contributing to our experiences with each other . . . knowing that each manifestation is of divine order and was, is, meant to be . . . to learn, teach, love and come to new awareness . . . that every Persons, Divine Beings, Angels, contribution is needed in the creation of what only really matters . . . and that is love . . .

VALENTINE'S DAY

*D*ear friends,

We can be stupid. We will fail. We, for a lack of a better word, are weird. But . . . that is okay. We also laugh at the most random things . . . some know my ugliest sides . . . because you took the time to really *see* me . . . Even though we disagree sometimes, we always overcome. When I am sad, you took the time to ask if I needed anything . . . and then hugged me . . . So sweet . . . So, what I am saying is . . . Thanks for sharing in my life . . .

I LOVE YOU

GUARDED HEARTS

I wrote this because I was pondering the relationships I have with others . . . and how we all guard our hearts from whatever *IT* is that holds us back . . . from expressing fully our heart desires...

$\mathcal{I}$ know that love can bring me back to center again when feeling unbalanced, skewed, tilted . . . I understand the truth that unconditional LOVE is the choice . . . a way to live my life to my fullest . . . creating my own path . . . that my experiences can be weaved and written in my heart . . . and are mine to entwine and create my stories with love . . . love is what carries me from one connection to another . . . observing, watching, noticing the unfolding of the Truths of my connections . . . coming to awareness of myself and having compassion for those I connect with . . . my eyes are being opened to new considerations . . . recognizing that there can be too much vulnerability to risk in softening one's guarded heart . . . I am finding my place . . . while patiently waiting, understanding, loving . . . only wishing the very best for those who, at times, are hiding in their self-imposed, fortified hearts . . . scared to take leaps of faith . . . Not fully trusting in self and others . . . to expose the most vulnerable parts of one's own heart . . . and accepting that we all are doing the best we can in our moments together . . . I choose to see the kindness, tenderness, gentleness, and love that is in all of us . . . I have nothing left to lose in surrendering to seeing the magic, light, loving . . . each person as we look for what we all want . . . to have the innocence, gentleness, tenderness, love, compassion, peace, joy, acceptance, TO BE SEEN WITHIN EACH OF US . . . knowing that love cannot be crushed, only hidden in guarded hearts...

WEIRD

This came about because someone told me they thought I was weird...

$\mathcal{W}$ e are blessed . . . I'm grateful for all those *weird* people . . . who dared to be uniquely different . . . and has and had the courage to stand out when it is and was safer to stand back . . . Our world is so much more beautiful . . . for the bravery creating ripple effects to show others . . . that they also can dare to be *weird* . . . . And shine...

YOU AND ME

This is the letter I wrote to my friend . . . about my expression of how I perceived our journey together . . . just now...

A Simple Truth . . . It is true . . . I love you...

More than I can say . . . this was not my intention to feel so deeply with you . . . it is the natural result of being totally open to sharing my guarded heart . . . It felt safe to do so . . . I understand that true intimacy is something that develops over time . . . trusting completely and sharing the deepest parts of self . . . I have come to awareness that intimacy is closeness in spirit, an unconditional love. It is more than an act . . . and it is more than pleasing words, it is the intention with which these actions and words are expressed . . . emotional intimacy entails being able to risk conflict . . . in order to move forward in a relationship. Risking sharing my heart at such an intimate level . . . brings the risks of experiencing the other person choices . . . understanding that there is the gift of loving and also understanding that loving, truly and deeply, is hard to absorb for others . . . and myself at times . . . Emotional intimacy is knowing that the relationship is secure enough . . . to share one's wholeness with another. Emotional intimacy embraces the other with tenderness, affection, trusting, and a willingness to share fully, growing, and supporting, and Surrendering to the Truths each has with God/ Universe/Self . . . and giving and receiving love, compassion, while staying in touch with the reality of who each person is or is not . . . just being who each was meant to be...

I want to be unbiased and not inflexible . . . express my love through tenderness, kindness, compassion . . . and not be apathetic to people around me . . . I want to be authentic and sincere in my communications . . . and not run when my ego is screaming at me to *see*, believe the stories, lies, coursing through my mind in those moments . . . So, what I guess I am coming to clarity on . . . is my true feeling for you . . . the definition of my feelings can be equated to what feelings are . . . experiences in giving and receiving unconditional love. I see our relationship as being untainted, kind, compassionate, and realistic with each other . . . I want to continue our relationship . . . however it unfolds naturally . . . and enjoy each other's company . . . because you let me be me . . . and accept me for who I am . . . a gift so rarely given . . . a gift I will treasure always . . . no matter your choices....

I will love you always and forever . . . for the beautiful, lovely, unique spirit you are . . . for showing me your tender heart at times . . . I see your flaws and love you all the more for them . . . I love you for simply Being . . . and I recognize how blessed I have been because we have intertwined . . .

P.S. The answer is found within and in our expression of ourselves for others to see . . . if willing to look, feel, love, act . . . Peace to you...

CLINGING

I wrote this after unwittingly still trying to control an outcome between my friend and me . . . I was afraid of not being accepted . . . I did not realize that I was acting out of my fear, yet again, about my self-worth . . . I did not trust the natural flow of our friendship or show trust in her love and acceptance of me . . . I wanted her to define the relationship instead of taking responsibility for my own happiness in the choices I make . . . I love my friend . . . so I have learned through this experience that this is all that truly matters . . . no matter her choices . . . I love her all the more . . . in her choices . . . trusting the natural flow . . . instead of trying to force, control, manipulate . . . creating an unintentional barrier . . . the opposite of what I was trying to do . . .

I went to bed with clarity of my actions and woke up with the gifts found in my actions. I am clinging at a level that I did not see before to people who love me dearly . . . my clinging is blocking the love to flow naturally . . . by me trying to be validated and re-assured I am loved. I recognize this is a form of controlling and forcing and is most unloving . . . and selfish . . . I am trying to remove responsibility from myself and trying to make others define my answers for me . . . so I cannot take responsibility for my actions . . . I also see that I do this when I become afraid and want to be loved and told I am going to be okay . . . instead I hide in my words . . . instead of just being honest and being seen for being afraid . . . you see, today I have to go and find out if the sores in my mouth that have not healed are cancer . . . I am scared . . . and I want to be seen and loved around my fear of

126

expressing that I am afraid, asking permission to share, and running into clinging . . . I see the action of not voicing my fears, and of fear not being seen, or rather cared about . . . and clinging has produced the one thing I don't want to do . . . and that is being unloving in my actions . . . and blocking the flow of love . . . .

Love, Love

TRYING TO CATCH MY BREATH . . .

Who knew that fracturing my wrist would bring my little girl in the forefront of my feelings? The most scared part of me . . . of feeling trapped . . . this is the only way I know how to express those fears of being afraid, caught, and unsure...

*T*here is a heaviness in my chest . . . trying to catch my breath . . . and I am not sure how I am going to pass through five weeks of feeling . . . all of this . . . I know I am not alone in this . . . yet I find myself, in moments, giving in to the little girl in me, that is so terrified . . . shivering, crying and praying, so scared of feelings of not being able to escape if need be . . . the little girl in me seems to not be able to hear or feel how safe we are . . . and loved . . . she is lost in her stories that appear to be evidence to support her fears of being trapped . . . and that the mom in me cannot protect her if mom is hurt . . . and no matter what my mom says to little girl, she cannot hear . . . or she forgets what she knows, feels . . . she wants to prove she is right in her fear . . . and wants everyone to pay attention because she truly believes the skewed evidence . . . she has collected as proof of her feelings . . . looking at all that evidence stored in her treasure box of memories . . . flashbacks . . . it's like being entombed in a room and watching a scary movie . . . and feeling so terrified of the demons that seemingly want to grab . . . and carry her away . . . to places unknown . . . and she feels no one is there to calm me down . . . and little girl is not well practiced at looking and seeing the truth . . . and knowing that she is safe and loved . . . the little girl in me is so busy throwing a tantrum . . . and she cannot seem to take a breath . . . and listen . . . not ready to let go quite yet . . . of the imaginary evidence . . . she wants to believe the mom in me . . . but she is too scared just now to entwine with her and feel safe . . . so the mom in me lets little girl feel her feelings instead of hiding them from her . . . mom knows it is time for little girl to explore and walk through the shadows . . . and be embraced fully in love . . . from all the parts of me . . . little girl also knows it is time . . . and she is scared . . . but she can see mom, and that she is patiently, lovingly, comforting her with her words, encouraging her to be brave enough . . . to fully feel all those scary, skewed feelings . . . and little girl knows that mom (all of me) is loved . . . because she has been watching mom with others . . . and can see, feel, how loved mom feels...

There Was A Little Girl...

The next two entries are about breaking my wrist dancing and having to have a cast put on. The cast triggered me into the fear of being trapped and unable to protect myself . . . turns out it was a gift . . . to look . . . see . . . feel . . . act . . . I learned that I am safe and loved and as I type this with my cast on my wrist, is just a mere inconvenience...

*T*here's a little girl who feels all by herself . . . feeling alone and scared . . . And though she smiles . . . there is something just hiding . . . and she struggles to find a way to connect . . . She feels unnoticed as life passes by . . . and she'll play make-believe to try to fill her up inside . . . when all she really wants is to cry . . . she'll say . . . please notice me . . . and see . . . I am scared to silence . . . And she would close her eyes . . . too afraid to speak her voice . . . reach out . . . and connect . . . just now . . . and mom is encouraging her to find courage to come and share . . . so the little girl paused and decided to trust and reach out . . .

Love, Love

Soul Awakening

I was listening to music while I was working . . . and this is what I was feeling, experiencing . . . In the moment . . . about my journey to finding me . . . the authentic me...

128

*H*ave you ever been distracted to awareness, carried to mindfulness, in moments in your day? Observing through your senses, seeing, hearing, smelling, tasting, touching, and flooding your consciousness with sensations, catching your attention . . . prompted to look, see, feel, act . . . chasing the fleeting moments that linger just around the corner of your next thoughts . . . observing the secret universe within you, that is in all of us . . . witnessing, all that is in those moments . . . memorized by the splendor . . . in a trance of the loveliness. And falling deeply into the feeling of grace, tenderness, kindness, love . . . embraced softly, comfortably in the arms of the phenomenon of the miracle of feeling . . . discovering just being . . . then something displays a part of your world, the places you have been, the people you love . . . a picture, a turn of phrase, a thought . . . flashes into focus to reminisce . . . moments . . . that seem frozen in time, in your mind, to revisit in those quite moments that seem so fleeting . . . of the intimate, spiritual connections, reunited, not limited by space or time, linked at the soul level, sensing the flow with others, what can only be described as divine grace, love . . . a soul awakening...

CLEVER TRICK

I wrote this on my lunch break . . . I was thinking of a friend . . . about when we slow down and just feel . . . and sometimes we are caught off guard by realizing we all have clever tricks...

*B*right Blue Eyes...with a twinkle in her eye, her melancholy smile exposes the uneasiness just below the surface . . . a clever trick . . . a revelation in the bright of day . . . wearing her heart on her sleeve . . . vulnerable, exposed, and feeling raw . . . centering on breathing throughout moments in her day . . . all the while her attention is pulled, in moments, to the insignificant voice, that lays within the rifts of her heart . . . that plays unceasingly, softly, and seems to crescendo in moments of doubt . . . her focus is drawn to the whisperings floating through her head for just an instant . . . long enough to plant the seeds of the uneasiness of the feeling that flashes through her for mere moments . . . causing discourse . . . coming to awareness . . . she recognizes Ego . . .

fighting for space in her consciousness . . . confronting her Soul, always teaching, reminding her, breathing softly, gently, unswervingly, that she is a divine Being, innocent, perfect in all that she is . . . quietly expressing to her to be patient . . . come to center . . . be kindhearted . . . compassionate . . . and there is no need to compete . . . or to feel small . . . there is nothing to be afraid of . . . and there is no longer a need to have feelings that she has to go without . . . that the world is not as far away as she seems to believe it is at times . . . that she has everything she needs already within her . . . and no need to be uneasy when she leaps . . . because in leaping she will learn to fly, to soar with her wings of courageousness, of love on the currents of the ripple effects of her making . . . to share with all others her soul . . . asking gently in those disbelieving moments of explorations within, "Don't you know how lovely you are . . . showing courage while learning, stumbling, crawling, connecting to love?

ANGELS IN DISGUISE

This piece came about after several conversations with friends . . . about who each of us are...

*W*ithin I can feel my soul stirring to a resilient consciousness . . . coming to the forefront, stirrings within to wakefulness, awareness . . . conscious . . . persistently, quietly, diligently, edging to the surface . . . with each shift . . . with each gift of awareness . . . I understand, observe, absorb, all that is . . . my truths of you and me . . . compassion, love for those who feel that they have to struggle alone, feeling separate, isolated, unwanted, having the sense of not mattering coursing through their illusions . . . skewed beliefs . . . because it feels safe to be in a familiar state . . . enduring, pushing through, head down against the winds of truth that sometimes are so resilient that one closes one's eyes to not *see*, feel, dream . . . and resisting the power of the truth . . . afraid of walking into the brightness, calmness of who each of us are . . . being responsible for the choice to *see* and contribute to our own happiness . . . in accountability to self . . . one will find the chains of outside perceptions slipping away . . . taking leaps of faith . . . gliding, soaring, to the choice of being authentic, really *seeing* the worth of self

130

and all others . . . embracing the beauty in each of us, the love, innocence . . . connected, creating ripple effects of energy bounding into the universe, our vibrations touching others, affecting each Being . . . when one comes to alignment with the truth of who we all are . . . Everyone a precious creation, with deep inner knowings, having a sense of unity when courageous enough to be vulnerable, exposed . . . to opening, softening of one's heart. A beginning, a transformation of the actuality which resonates from all of us who we are . . . that we are incarnate in human form to raise the vibration of the world, to radiate . . . each Being an Angel in Disguise...

LIGHT UP

I wrote this after spending time talking with two lovely young ladies who are coming into womanhood . . . one being my daughter, the other part of the Real Love community I belong to . . .

*L*ight up and shine. Beautiful girl . . . Beautiful smile . . . Beautiful soul....

You are wonderful . . . just as you are . . . with a twinkle in your eye . . . When talking about your passions . . . heart desires . . . you naturally light up . . . with music in your laughter . . . and your smile sparkles, radiates when you beam in your natural beauty . . . and the world is a little brighter . . . as your presence is a gift to the world...

You are uniquely brilliant, a child of God . . . meant to let your light shine, to illuminate the world . . . to touch and inspire others . . . connecting, sharing . . . in unconditional love . . . You are resilient . . . even when you, at times, don't feel that way . . . finding new adventures, with each choice made by you, which contribute to your happiness . . . you will naturally light up as you move forward in your life journey . . . creating your own miracles . . . finding the answers through your personal experiences . . . stretching, growing...

Unwrapping the gifts found in the treasure of being *YOU* . . . a heart full of creativity, kindness, curiosity, generosity, bravery, softness . . . love . . . glowing outwardly . . . your spirit thriving through everything you do . . . your inner bliss spilling out, and your enthusiasm, your zest

131

for life . . . an inspiration . . . to us all as we watch . . . you are beautiful...

There is no wrong way to walk your path . . . just choices in the bends and bumps you will experience . . . as you listen to your inner voice . . . heart . . . you will discover your dreams can come true . . . and your attitude will determine how you will feel . . . walk your journey . . . when you BELIEVE in YOU . . . your world will open up to unexplored possibilities...

My wish for you is to have the COURAGE to DREAM BIG . . . DARE to take LEAPS OF FAITH and not be afraid to DARE . . . that YOU KNOW INHERENTLY YOUR WORTH and that YOU ARE LOVED BEYOND MEASURE . . . and to ALWAYS remember that when you are naturally being you . . . The world is GRACED WITH YOUR INNER BEAUTY when you LIGHT UP...

Love you to the moon and back ♥

Love, Love

COMMONPLACE FAIRY TALE

I was sitting at my desk thinking about how routine life can become when "falling asleep," not being aware . . . and going into auto-pilot . . . then I started listening to the lyrics of the song I was listening to and realized we all have parts of fairy tales in our everyday lives when we stop, see, feel . . . in our commonplace, ordinary, typical life...

*T*hrough your ordinary days . . . that sometimes kinda feel like a commonplace fairy tale . . . when nothing seems to have any rhyme or reason . . . when looking, feeling fragmented . . . feeling like there is a missing piece of your heart, and trying once again to fit in . . . guarding your self-described shattered heart . . . trying to put your heart puzzle pieces together again . . . hungry to be a part of all that is . . . may your thoughts drift to knowing that you are loved . . . when dealing with the details of everyday life . . . recognizing that your flaws make you more beautiful then all your perfections . . . know that you are not alone . . . a natural influence, full of magic, when you daydream and your eyes reveal all of who are . . . making believers out of disbelievers in their ordinary, everyday, fairy tale lives . . . charmed, entranced, enchanted endlessly, and very nearly always with the light, spirit, love, radiating from within you, shining, creating connections . . . and in those moments may you be blessed to *see* and come to awareness of the beauty within yourself and others . . . and understand that an everyday, ordinary, commonplace fairy tale can also be full of magic . . . when each of us stop to look, see, feel, act . . . with a knowing . . . of all each of us are . . . a gift, treasure, and talent . . . A contribution . . . uniquely self . . . yet connected . . . when sharing in our commonplace fairy tale...

INNER STRENGTH

I found myself unable to sleep and tossing and turning . . . so I wrote this to express my feelings of fear of having to do my scans to check for cancer . . . to the Real Love Goddess Group I belong to . . . I wanted to be *seen* in this moment . . . to connect and reach out...

S ometimes the unexpected happens . . . and it can be such a journey . . . an undertaking that can drive one to the edge . . . we have to choose to believe in our own inner strength . . . and understand the truth . . . that we have the courage and bravery to overcome our personal fears . . . that we can conquer the distress, anxiety, worry, that can stir within us . . . when looking at the illusions that make up our story . . . a fabled falsehood that can lead us to being distracted from *seeing* all of who each of us are . . . our true essence . . . instead, we turn away from SELF and get lost in the details of our familiar every day happenings . . . missing what is expressed with each connection, encounter with others...

We create our own magic, reality through our choices . . . we choose how we live in our world . . . linking with one another, supporting, encouraging, accepting, loving . . . as each of us walk our chosen path to experience . . . ALL that we . . . understanding we are doing the best we can . . . Ever evolving consciously or unconsciously . . . experiencing the blessings that are shown to us . . .

When we stop . . . to look . . . listen . . . feel . . . to experience, elevate to awareness of a knowing . . . of unconditional acceptance . . .

unconditional love . . . sharing in the universal vibration . . . creating ripple effects from the choices made . . . influencing, touching, embracing All others . . . prompting, encouraging waves of gratitude . . . flowing outwardly . . . gently, softly, immersing and inspiring . . . to rise up and create momentum . . . to leap and overcome . . . and fly into the AMAZING BEAUTY . . . in choosing to have fearlessness in the flight inward to an open heart ...

WICKEDLY LOVELY

I just started writing . . . this is what came out of my thoughts . . . about my past year or so of being on the path I chose to go down and explore . . . never could I have imagined my life as it is today...

I thought before I was fulfilled, satisfied, okay . . . not really . . . just convinced myself to believe in the illusions of my ordinary every day routines . . . day dreaming of possibilities . . . as I could not believe this is all that there was to living . . . loving . . . my blue skies fading to gray . . . falling to pieces . . . and my visions, when shared, discounted, not taken seriously, being laughed at . . . for the imaginings I shared. I, always responding, with a giggle and a shrug of the shoulders and a painted on smile . . . going along for the ride . . . questioning me . . . continuously telling myself . . . "It's not time yet" . . . and gradually I learned not to share with anyone else . . . not daring or feeling any longer . . . My dreams and I endlessly drifting farther and farther apart . . . each time feeling a little bit more alone . . . getting lost in the details of life...

Then an angel appeared in my life . . . accepting me, patiently teaching me with compassion and unconditional love . . . coaching me to see *me* . . . teaching me how to embrace myself, my worth, value . . . that I have a gift to contribute to the world . . . that we all have gifts, and each of us matter. As I embraced and practiced my life lessons, I naturally grew to share my love with others openly . . . the natural consequence of choosing happiness over controlling, adjusting, modifying myself . . . to feel accepted . . . no longer creating illusions of me . . . just authentically, genuinely, vulnerably being me...

So freeing, being comfortable in my own skin, container, vessel . . . at times feeling so very deeply, compassion for all , loving , caring, showing tenderness, kindness, continually awe-inspired by those who weave and twine with me in my life . . . it has increased my understandings . . . creating new depths of who *we all are* . . . adding layers to my perception, sensitivity, mindfulness, tenderness, and the power of unconditional love . . . creating calmness and peace within me . . . with awareness of the gift of love, by choosing to travel the road less voyaged . . . and in choosing to do so . . . the pathway has opened to new encounters . . . having a *knowing* that it is never too late to make choices that contribute to my happiness . . . that I have the power within me to choose . . . to be stuck in my fears and lies or find the courage to take leaps of faith . . . moving forward . . . My heart is lighter, brighter . . . life is a little bit more luminous . . . and to me . . . that is just . . . so, so, very lovely, exquisite, such a beautiful way to see me, you, all of us . . . I would say . . . "Not a Beautiful Mess, but rather wickedly lovely"...

CHERISH AND LOVE

Today I decided that this would be where I would complete the sharing of my thoughts for now . . . I still have my blog and web site I can share on . . . there is so much recently flooding my senses, creating new thoughts, feelings, and urging me to keep sharing . . . and I will . . . this last entry is for ALL of YOU...

I LOVE YOU...

*T*o Those I Cherish and Love,

I wanted to take a moment in time . . . and stop the world for you . . . to recognize you for all that you are . . . the radiance from within you shining brightly . . . manifesting in life through your willingness to be open, vulnerable in sharing your voice, your heart . . . contributing to the world through your ripple effects . . . Of being courageous, brave . . . to take leaps of faith . . . thank you for *seeing* and embracing the world with open arms. To experience life, all that it offers, and the people you touch through giving and receiving love, tenderness, kindness, compassion, and passion. Your presence is noticed and touches others to

135

look, see, feel, and act in love to begin the softening of hearts . . . spreading vibrations of grace, peace, love , through you being you . . . living authentically, with an open nature and spirit . . . you may not see or notice your impact, influence, guidance on others . . . inspiring, encouraging in unconditional love. I wanted to let you know that I *see* you, and I understand that your presence matters, that you are important, and all that you contribute to life is a blessing . . . and I, we, the Universe, would not be the same if you were not a part . . . I love you to the moon and back . . . and even more deeply & simply . . . you are in my heart . . .

Love, Love

FOREVER AND ALWAYS

I need to include this last writing . . . it is my perspective of all that I walked through in my marriage, and of growing into who I am now . . . understanding we all need room to be authentically unique individuals . . . and there is no right or wrong way to *BE* . . . just choices . . . on our journey within . . . discovering who we are . . . LOVE

*J*n this farewell to the forever and always we were a part of . . . Knowing always that we each hold love for the other . . . we go our separate ways with treasures collected to reminisce . . . lessons learned . . . one with a heart more open . . . the other feeling heart wounded . . . uncertain, and still confused . . . not understanding the choices made by the other . . . defining love and happiness differently . . . saying good-bye to what we fought so hard to keep . . . the struggle . . . heartache, turning my back on the expectations of how we defined what love is and is not . . . unraveling, untwining, all that seemed so important and now feels like a fragment of me . . . us . . . a moment in time . . . looking back and feeling all experienced . . . was in the blink of an eye . . . and observing and confessing that I never gave "all of me" . . . choosing instead to just live in an illusion with you . . . chasing fruition of what was expected created through our own self-seeking views, supported by those that flowed in and out of our lives . . . always sharing what *should* be . . . how one *ought* to be . . . we just kept ignoring ourselves, in fear, afraid to just *BE* who each of us are . . . feeling isolated, dying from the inside out . . . feeling empty . . . unwanted . . . not seen or heard . . . convincing ourselves that contentment was a space to strive for and stay in . . . unconsciously creating an emotional abyss . . . that when finally acknowledged . . . could no longer be disregarded . . . the distance seemed so vast . . . neither of us any longer willing to jump and run through the depths of our self-created chasm . . . of emotions . . . both of us becoming lost . . . each of us blinded by selfish needs and wants . . . in these choices we only stagnated, resisted, fighting our natural urges to be authentically human, individualistic, and comfortable in our own skin . . . instead we built and fortified our inner walls with skewed beliefs of one another, clinging, attacking, running and lying, not seeing the beauty, loveliness, uniqueness and gifts that each is . . . and how each does contribute matters, and is important . . . and I now *see* with clarity that we both have the chance, a gift, to "wake up" from our self-subscribed, limiting dream we called our truth . . . and come back to reality . . . stop taking and defining for others . . . and discover new possibilities . . . we can choose to breathe . . . relax . . . observe . . . feel . . . explore . . . and act in the capacity in which we decide . . . and believe . . . in our inner truths that speak, whisper to us, in those quite moments, of who each of us really are . . . our purpose, our genuine truth . . . that each of us are loved and are love . . . that each person has the ability to be a presence that gives from the heart, with the capability to be courageous enough, to be vulnerable, exposed, authentic . . . finding bravery to share in compassion, kindness, tenderness, gentleness, mindfulness . . . creating peace from the inside out . . . accepting others . . . And understanding with certainty that each of us are doing the best we can in every moment . . . growing and expanding, learning, teaching with others . . . and each day on this side of reality, the universe, a blessing . . . as I truly believe that you and I and ALL others . . . contribute to the universal vibration . . . creating ripple effects of our choosing . . . *Forever and Always...*

GOOD-BYE

S aying good-bye . . . my feelings run to all the good-byes I chose to say . . . sometimes for me . . . and sometime for them . . . doesn't matter how the good-byes come to be . . . although there is anticipation for what lies ahead . . . there are those soft, beautiful, lovely moments in our hearts . . . that bring us to those tears . . . Tears of love . . . and knowing that moments together can seem fleeting at times . . . and understanding how blessed we are to have the chance to twine and re-twine in the recollecting of shared instances . . . with those we love . . . that brings us to a silently reverie . . . Shining through our Beings . . . sharing in the smiles of those treasured moments . . . And in moments sharing outwardly . . . to create ripple effects of love offered freely in those memories...

We are on a journey to find who we are . . . We seem to dream . . . about taking leaps of faith . . . to follow our hearts . . . our inner voice . . . When aware, asking for guidance as to what is meant to be . . . To find the strength, courage, and bravery to leap . . . listen . . . act . . . love . . . creating ripple effects . . . To teach others to dream . . . and to *see* the love within . . . creating courage to also leap . . . and create more ripple effects...

Watching our children and others walk their path . . . making choices . . . taking leaps of faith . . . can and does take bravery, courage, unconditional love, and Breathing . . . with those who love, those who leap . . . understanding that our loved ones are compelled to listen to their voice...

Untwining . . . unwrapping the gift of saying good-bye . . . Just uttering those words can bring me to tears . . . because understanding the connection, our children's everyday presence will be no more . . . not hearing their voices, giggles, laughter, or sharing every day occurrences like the way they smell when hugged. And knowing that the gift of sharing their heart wrenching and most loving moments will not be ours to open first . . . because as our children expand and grow in love, it naturally will include others . . . And the realization that our kids are who they are because of who we are . . . being authentically human . . . brings tears of happiness to my eyes because I can see the manifestation of the ripple effects of our creation . . . shining through our children . . .

FINAL THOUGHTS

*W*hen I finally made the choice to contribute to my happiness by *leaning in* . . . and trusting my worth . . . and all people's worth . . . it became very clear to me . . . I know that each of us matters, and are important . . . and each of us are worth stopping the world for . . . and that all paths lead to unconditional love.

Through the Real Love books, I discovered the Real Love Community . . . This is where I met Sharon . . . and I learned from her that love does leave a significant mark . . . and nothing will ever be the same again...

Know that you are loved beyond measure . . . and are love . . . and you have a purpose . . . surrender . . . and let your light shine . . . to share with others . . . we are all blessed, and I am honored, grateful, and humbled that you shared in my heart songs . . . peace be with you until our paths cross again...

In Closing I am going to share a writing I set to music. It is simply called, "I AM"...

"I AM"

I had a dream . . . that I could be just me and fly away into my visions . . . that are continually, gracefully affecting my reality . . . Soaring with the wind of change . . . gently caressing my face. And stroking a soft wind across my form . . . increasing, embracing, encouraging, the day dreams . . . flowing, listening intently . . . Feeling Deeply in the center of me . . . to hear the message found in the knowings of the truth within me . . . IN ALL of US . . . the conscious awareness . . . releasing my thoughts and drifting . . . to *see* visibly . . . the pathway . . . connecting with others . . . when our eyes encounter . . . joining, in those moments, recognizing I AM experiencing, linking with the expression of God/Universe/Source . . . shining forth from within others . . . INSPIRED BY LOVE I just breathe and . . . I melt into LOVE with a knowing . . . that we are ALL a manifestation of LOVE . . . and I become sensitive to Being . . . in the presence of God/Universe/Source . .

139

. Soaring in the currents of ripple effects of my making . . . through the intentions of my thoughts . . . understanding the Blessings we each have and share . . . to choose to *see* or *not see* . . . to hear life's songs . . . humming, streaming, coursing, moving through me . . . through each of us . . . To dance on life's dance floor . . . to follow the rhythms, to interact with the pulses that wash over us . . . to absorb, sharing, creating energy, identifying THE PURPOSE, each of us are here to experience in . . . sharing . . . creating waves of . . . consciousness of our own making . . . our essence weaving with others to TEACH, LEARN, GROW, EXPAND . . . sharing our passions of COMPASSION, TENDERNESS, KINDNESS . . . BEING COURAGEOUS, BRAVE, VULNERABLE . . . to SPEAK and LIVE OUR TRUTHS . . . listening to our inner voice.... whispering softly . . . prompting us to NOT HIDE . . . to come to AWARENESS . . . of who each of us are . . . that each of us matter . . . each of us are important . . . and the UNIVERSE . . . would be less than without each person's contribution to the universal vibration . . . Listening . . . being in tune with SELF to hear . . . to feel the murmurings from within . . . swaying each of us to embrace . . . love who each of us are . . . and in doing so . . . we will find . . . FREEDOM, JOY, ACCEPTANCE . . . coming to love ourselves and others and . . . to be gentle with ourselves as we stumble, crawl toward awakenings, awareness of ALL of who each of us are . . . All the while being nudged by our inner spirit to *see* through the illusions of our minds . . . inspiring us to . . . STOP, LISTEN, LOOK, ACT on our heart stirrings . . . to a deeper understanding of . . . all that we are and all that I AM...

I AM LOVE

I AM GRACE

I AM KINDNESS

I AM COMPASSION

I AM TENDERNESS

I AM PEACE

I AM JOY

I AM VULNERABLE

I AM BLESSED

And…

I AM ME….

Simply…

I AM

And…

I AM YOU

Intertwined throughout the eternities…

LETTERS FROM MY
FAMILY AND FRIENDS

A PERSPECTIVE OF BARBARA (ME!)

I thought long and hard about including these letters with my writings . . . Mostly, because when I requested that a few people from my life give his or her understanding, perspective of me, my intention was to show parts of me that I may not even be aware of, or maybe I should say I've ignored . . . I am humbled, and once again have learned and grown from each letter . . . that love is all that really matters . . . the rest is just details . . . and will fade away into ambiguity . . . At the end of the day, I know my heart, my love, for each and every person . . . and more so with those that I am blessed to have twined in my world . . .

I hope that each person who takes the time to share in my journey will understand how these parts of me, the pieces of my heart, have and has touched and shifted me, to new understandings of awareness . . . what I simply call, a *Beautiful Mess...*

A LETTER FROM DRAKE - MY TRIPLET BROTHER

*E*veryone has heroes in life, and for me, one of those heroes is my sister, Barbara. She's my hero for many reasons, but first and foremost she's my hero because she has impeccable character, competencies only a few possess, and a love for life rarely seen in those who have gone through the battles she has. Growing up, I would observe her often, and I secretly wanted to be like her. She always did things of benefit to others, and made the best of any situation. Even though I am sure some of those situations had an adverse effect on her, I never once saw her show it. The best thing about Barbara is she continues to be herself, day in and day out.

My earliest memory of Barbara was when I was four years old and my brother, Todd, was born. Due to a number of complications during his delivery, and having been diagnosed as bipolar, my mother was unable to do much of anything. My father was out of the picture, and because my mother was ill, she always needed help. My sister stepped up and did most of the things that my mother was unable to do. She took care of my other sister, one great brother, and me, as well as any mother could have. She did this throughout our adolescent years, and I'm sure if it were not for her, I would not be where I am today – with a life of happiness and fulfillment.

I always knew Barbara was a great human being, but when life threw her the biggest curve ball one could face, Cancer; she really proved how wonderful and amazing she truly is. I recall the day she shared the news and how she was determined to turn a difficult situation into an opportunity to develop herself and other people.

It seems like it happened in the blink of an eye, but time has flown by for Barbara and I, and now nearing fifty years into it, I'm fortunate to have her in my life. I will try to be as wonderful a person as she is.

Simply put . . . I love my sister, and she is my hero. She is simply amazing and I just couldn't imagine life without her.

With all my love and respect,

Drake

A LETTER FROM FAYE - MY TRIPLET SISTER

$\mathcal{W}$ e have shared many paths together:

Learning from each other, supporting each other, understanding each other, knowing that you are a part of me, and I, a part of you.

I am grateful for the soul connection that entwines us; the opportunity to share this lifetime with you. To see you grow and explore, to grow into awareness through the stages of our lives. To be the observer of your experiences is awe inspiring.

You lead by example; I see that you are not afraid to stop the world that is spinning around you, to reflect and learn from your experiences, to be able to understand the lessons to be learned, and the willingness to pave a path so that others may follow. You do not give up on yourself when barriers arise; you forge ahead and blaze a new trail if necessary, even it means going around the mountain to continue on your path. It is an honor to have you as my sister and as a teacher.

I know you to be true to yourself, knowing your purpose, and able to share the essence of who you are.

Now is the moment, and who you are in this moment is what is important. To be able to say to the world:

I know who I am, I know what I am,

I know how I serve.

(The last three lines are from Paul Silig)

These are the lessons to learn, and once learned, to share with others.

Faye

A LETTER FROM ERIN G - MY CO-WORKER

My Barb Story

*W*hen I first met Barb, I felt she was closed off and shy. She didn't get involved in much conversation and she hid herself away. When I spoke with her one day, I realized there was a beautiful, caring, sweet lady hidden inside her. As the years went on, we only knew each other superficially, until one day she shared a personal battle she was fighting with me. I saw she was scared, nervous, and alone. We spoke for quite a long time and I wished her the best – and I meant it. Barb gave me updates as she could, and I always looked forward to seeing her or hearing from her. One day we shared similar personal news with each other. An instant bond formed and what transpired changed my perceptions of this woman forever. She looked brighter, lighter, and dare I say . . . happy. Her eyes lit up as she spoke about love, faith, and hope for the future. I almost didn't recognize her as the Barb I had known for the past 5 years. This woman was strong, confident, and vibrant. Barb finally understood herself and love; she had discovered her passion. Her energy radiates from her now as she talks about her experiences and her feelings. She shares herself with everyone – even people she's just met. She cares for people entirely. I can listen to her speak and never get bored. Barb has a way of making people feel they are not alone. Barb changed my life when I was in need of a friend. She held my hand and offered me her – just her – and that was enough. She may not change the world, but she certainly changed mine.

Much love to you sister!

Erin G.

SHARON A. WINNINGHAM, CRLC . . .

My Certified Real Love Coach

Bold.

Dynamic.

Precious and Vulnerable.

*S*he had no idea who she was. Barbara Heite is an angel and one in a million. Her truly unique way of seeing light in everything with grace and gratitude makes her unstoppable in any adventure she takes on. She has an amazing spirit to persevere through times that would have others fall to their knees.

She loves with all her heart and has learned only recently that she is important, because of that. There is no other word for her but LOVE.

Sharon A. Winningham

FINAL THOUGHTS

AND FINALLY, ME...
SHARING THOUGHTS ON FINDING MYSELF

*G*oing deeper into finding, seeing, me . . . exploring . . . how much parts of me fight to be in the driver seat of my life (soul) . . . always positioning, manipulating my true self . . . causing turmoil and questioning . . . I have come to the point where I understand this is no longer productive and I understand that I am standing in my own way . . . the parts in me that have developed over my life experiences are here, in me, to protect me from the pain that is so well protected . . . it is how I have internalized and rationalized with myself . . . parts of me frozen in time . . . in those moments of trauma . . . with good reason . . .

Those child-like parts of me are in fear of being abandoned and not surviving. Those parts of me are desperate to be saved, and will cling to any hope and to anyone who offers help. The adult parts that are so protective of my child-like parts are committed to not letting others close for fear of being hurt again . . . and there are parts that if hurt, want to rage, and can become engulfed in a silent fury over the injustices of the pain endured by the vulnerable child-like parts. Then there are the parts of me that want to manage and control everything . . . being manipulative and coercive . . . all the while functioning at a high level through the details of life . . . very efficient . . . vigilant . . . always looking for evidence to reinforce those injustices and proof of belief . . . very in tune to shifts in people's moods . . . and creative and extremely sensitive.

I have come to understand that I have spent my life trying to get rid of those parts of me that I don't like . . . rigidly banning them . . . which works for a while . . . then those parts of me would regroup and come back even stronger . . . and those parts feel so resilient, and force and hijack the driver seat of me . . . taking over the core authentic self . . . making harsh, rash decisions that would have been different if not for the fear of being abandoned, ignored, rejected . . . and my true self was not strong enough to reason and separate from those extreme emotions and thoughts . . . I was stunned into silence . .

. and unsure of what to do . . . losing control of those emotions and thoughts...

I am committed to finding the bravery to explore those parts of me I have been afraid of, in fear of, to really look at them . . . until fairly recently . . . I am becoming more and more aware of my inner strength and worth and I can sense the feelings of those parts of me, and acknowledge the outlooks, stances of those parts, understanding that those parts of me just want to be seen and accepted and acknowledged with love and with compassion. If I can remember to approach those feelings (parts) with softness, tenderness, gentleness, this calms those emotions of fear . . . which allows constructive healthy communication, and to ask the questions to explore without anger, defensiveness, or self-dislike. It is an opportunity to discover, understand, and acknowledge in an internal atmosphere of acceptance . . . knowing that each voice (emotion) is important, matters, and can contribute to my essential happiness . . . this leads to a feeling of stillness, honesty, serenity, and a willingness to be vulnerable . . . connecting with the most delicate, innocent and exposed aspects of me . . . finding the capacity to experience joyfulness, love, creativeness, musings, light heartiness, adventures and spirit . . . finding clarity . . . embracing my true identity, essence, Being . . . with a knowing of my worth . . . And to cultivate an internal environment of safety and unconditional love . . . to have the courage to make choices that will lead to my happiness through sharing all parts of me with an open heart . . . and to listen within . . . as this is where the healing will be completed . . . not outward but inward . . . Traveling within to explore the Universe twirling inside me . . . weaving, twining, ever evolving into what I call . . . a Beautiful Mess...

Welcome to my heart . . . I am so honored and humbled and grateful for each moment shared with you . . . traveling on the path of finding me and discovering you . . . I am . . . and we all are . . . Blessed...

Love, Love

RESOURCES...

To learn more about Real Love, and to order books and services created by the author, Greg Baer:

www.Reallove.com

To get in touch with Sharon Winningham, a Certified Real Love Coach with over eight years of experience in coaching, available in person or via skype around the world:

www.sharonwinningham.com

swinningham@reallove.com

Barb Heite

www.Lovebarbloveu.com

Amordesoi2@gmail.com

Amor De Soi
7349 Via Paseo Del Sur
Suite 515;PO Box 195
Scottsdale AZ 85258